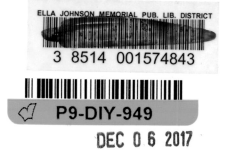

THE CLOSEST
I'VE COME

THE CLOSEST I'VE COME

FRED ACEVES

HARPER TEEN

An Imprint of HarperCollinsPublishers

HarperTeen is an imprint of HarperCollins Publishers.

Library of Congress Control Number: 2017943589
ISBN 978-0-06-248853-4

Typography by Fine Design
17 18 19 20 21   PC/LSCH   10 9 8 7 6 5 4 3 2 1
❖
First Edition

For my sisters, Yesmin and Stefany, because during the
mystifying journey through childhood
I was never completely alone.

AT SCHOOL I'm a boss. In baggy jeans and a tee, with swaggy slowness and an icy stare, I roam the halls with my boys.

Other kids shoulder backpacks, talk in twos or threes. Some thumb at cell phones, rocking new clothes they got over Christmas break: sneakers with that store gleam, no fuzz on their sweaters and hoodies.

Guys call out to their friends, giving quick chin raises, while the girls shriek and run smiling to each other's arms, squeezing like twin sisters reunited after war.

What I notice most are the couples. Ain't many holding hands and ain't none kissing so far but you can spot them, their side-by-side walk with that matching rhythm or how they stand super close to talk.

When's *my* turn? Never had me a girlfriend and seems like I never will, which has at least something to do with being broke.

Today I'm looking less ratty than normal with my new solid black tee, a Christmas present. With four tees I used to repeat the same one on Monday and Friday. Now, for my final sophomore semester, I got five in rotation.

Coming up on us is a suited man, fiftyish and lean, the smoke-colored hair from the sides plastered over the bald spot.

"Hello there." He comes to a stop and smiles, hands in his pockets. His breezy way tells me he might be the one actually running things here. Probably the new principal.

"Hi," I say, with two friends joining in.

The man nods. "You guys look dangerous."

I thank him and we keep moving.

In homeroom I dig into my pocket for some pebbles and start plinking them against a side window. Whenever old and half-deaf Mrs. Howard notices, she asks for the "disruptive activity" to stop.

Uppercut in front of me is checking out the kid who screwed up bad last year and wore an Iron Man tee, freshman mistake, and has been "Virginboy" ever since. "Hey, Virginboy," he says now, and laughs when the kid looks over.

Uppercut lives in my hood and I guess we sorta friends. He's down for me, like when I got jumped behind the Sweetbay, and joined my boys in our search for the guys who did it. But I don't trust him, don't actually like him.

This is a guy who slams into others in the halls on purpose.

With nothing but roll call during homeroom he's got time to make fun of people.

Skinny Tim, who sits in front of Uppercut, is "Whiney-bitch." Whenever Uppercut punches him during the Pledge of Allegiance, the kid lets out a low groan.

Areli with the horse pencil case, who's nice to everybody, is "Churchgirl."

Super-smart Melissa is "Fatfuck."

Amy, a punk girl who sticks out more than anybody—blue streaks in her brown hair, eye-catching clothes—is safe way on the other side of the classroom.

I gotta admit she looks cool with that hair, the tagged-up green Chucks, the jangly bracelets and slashed jeans she sometimes wears. Other rocker-type girls here seem to be all image, like last week they was still into Barbies and cartoons.

Uppercut, pimpled and with a broken front tooth, sporting ATR kicks and that Puerto Rican flag shirt, is an easy target. And dissing him is a great idea if you love catching a beatdown in public.

Lucky me Uppercut's my sorta friend.

SLAP! Right on my forehead.

"Stop spacing, Marcos," Uppercut says.

I rub the spot and remind myself that slaps ain't no reason to get pissed, even if they do hurt like hell. Girls can nice each other to death all day, give out compliments and hugs, snap group selfies everywhere they go, but boys gotta take swings and call each other bitches.

Don't ask me. I don't make the rules.

The prehistoric loudspeaker over the whiteboard crackles and hums. Then comes the electric screech, warning that somebody in the front office is about to talk.

"Attention, Hanna High students." It's the man from the hall. He introduces himself as Principal Perry, and though we want to hear more about last semester's scandal—the sexts the last principal sent to at least three girls—he just welcomes us back like it's normal to switch principals midschool year.

The secretary handles the yawnfest announcements, the date and time of open house, PTA meetings, and spelling bees. When the principal's on we all ears.

After telling us how happy he is to be here, he says, "Anyone in violation of the dress code be warned . . ."

We know the dress code. No short skirts or shorts (for the girls) and no sagging pants or shirts with drug references (for the boys).

A few guys sport marijuana leaf tees. If caught, you gotta wear the shirt inside out, 'cause in this school a leaf's distracting but clothes worn the wrong way ain't.

"Let me be clear," Principal Perry says. "Clothing or jewelry with suggestive or questionable language or drawings may not be worn. Examples include, but are not limited to: gang-related symbols; racial, ethnic, or sexual slogans or innuendoes; images or language about drugs, alcohol, or tobacco. Also, anyone wearing sagging pants will be immediately punished from now on."

Me and Uppercut eye each other.

An emo kid pounds a fist on his desk. "Fucking shit!"

Principal Perry clears his throat like he heard. "Dresses, skirts, and shorts must extend beyond the students' fingertips when their arms are held to the sides."

I check out Amy on the other side of the room, at what I can see of her short black skirt. Everybody's looking at her.

Though her stick legs ain't nothing to whistle at, she's cuter than some of the other girls around here.

I ain't never had sex, which has me crazy horny and thinking about it nonstop. Mall mannequins can excite me and surprise boners pop up during class, making me wonder what the hell's going on down there.

But I swear sex ain't the most important thing. It'd be dope just kicking it with a girl. Ain't females the greatest ever? Tell your problems to a girlfriend and she don't make fun of you. A girlfriend means you ain't alone.

"Have a wonderful day, Hanna High students," Perry says, his voice getting swallowed up by the ear-shattering screech. They tell us our loud headphones will damage our hearing and then make us sit through this noise.

The last principal also signed off the same way, called us "Hanna High students" like we a sports team or fan club, not a bunch of kids herded together 'cause we live close by. What else we got in common besides the same teachers, lunch food, and homework? What do I share with perfect-life Kyle Benson sitting up front?

I used to get on the school computer to sorta stalk him. Checked out his pages, his posts and pics, read the comments—blond Kyle who goes out with Tina. He's such a pretty boy you wanna punch him in the face, and she's such a hottie you wanna punch yourself in the face.

A search brought up lots of pics, even an old baseball one, small Kyle uniformed at home plate, ready to swing, bat pointing to the sun. Newer pics were taken in restaurants, a paintball field, outside the AMC theater.

That kid don't kick it like me and my boys. He's got *activities*. One thousand, eight hundred and eighty-five pics of proof on his Instagram, last I checked, while my no-credit phone don't even got a camera.

Ask me if his posts make me jealous and I gotta admit that yeah, just a little. Even the stuff he complained about was dope. Once he posted, *stuck @ fam reunion*.

Done with attendance, Mrs. Howard now calls Amy's name again. "Come here, please."

Amy shifts in her seat, hands tugging and wiggling the skirt down. When she stands up you can see her skirt's gone longer, the top hugging the bottom of her butt, and her Misfits tee covering up the trick. We watch her skinny legs move toward the teacher's desk.

Mrs. Howard sets her reading glasses halfway down her nose. "Extend your arms and no shrugging."

As Amy stands there, fingers reaching down to touch her skirt, she turns her head to smile at us.

That confidence in front of twenty-plus pairs of eyes could be real. Though we sophomores here, Amy rolls with some juniors and seniors, which tops the cool meter. Rockers, artsy kids, and other weirdos, a tiny but rowdy group that share a table in the cafeteria and cigarettes behind the gym.

I ain't never seen her smile before now. It's a nice smile.

Mrs. Howard removes her glasses. "Very well."

As we all try not to laugh, Amy's grin goes wider on the way to her seat. We all sharing a moment for the first time. If our teacher's ears were better she'd hear the snorts and giggles escaping us.

Amy's trick was even better than most of the stuff I get away with.

When Uppercut's head turns to me, I know it's coming. I just hope Amy don't hear it.

He says, "That bitch is skinnier than a crack whore."

Two girls giggle.

Amy backs up a few steps to stand in front of the classroom again, hands on hips. A straight mouth has replaced the grin. "You got something to say?"

All heads turn to us in back. Mrs. Howard slides her

eyes from Amy to Uppercut and back, not getting it.

Just one word comes outta Uppercut—"What?"

"Don't *even*. Unlike you, I spoke up, you chickenshit."

Damn! Amy's as fearless as the girls who live in my hood, Maesta.

Uppercut glances around all slow like he's about to lean forward to look at someone's test answers. "Sit down and shut the hell up."

Still in front of the class she says, "You talk and talk, dude, but you never say anything."

Sitting behind him, there ain't no way to see his face. Is he pissed? Embarrassed? I'm expecting some sorta comeback, but punk girl's on a roll.

"Forever talking about who's fat or skinny or dorky, but what's so great about *you*?"

Nothing, I answer in my head, feeling a combo of excited and scared. I want Amy to stand up there forever, to never stop talking. Someone please give her a megaphone! Her own TV show! I also sorta hope she sits down and shuts up so Uppercut don't start dissing her. Or worse.

I *could* tell Uppercut to chill but he's thick from lifting weights, could snap me like a toothpick. Once he knocked out his own cousin for trying to stop a fight. One punch was all it took.

"Young lady, you need to sit down!" Mrs. Howard's pointing in case Amy forgot which seat. "Sit down this moment!"

Amy's eyes stay locked on Uppercut. "You're a shitbag, making fun of others to make yourself feel better."

He says, "Shut up, bitch."

A few girly gasps fly through the air but the guys' faces just hang there.

Dammit! Amy's walking over here! Such a dumb move. I could get up, keep her away from Uppercut, or tell him to leave her alone. I know I should, but the truth is, I ain't tough. Even with guys my age and size who start shit. I'd rather walk away. It's why I only been in seven fights my whole life.

Amy comes down our row and right up to Uppercut who gets on his feet. He's half a head taller. They practically breathing on each other.

"Wanna make me?" A gangster stare like she's ready for all-out war.

My heart speeds up even more.

"Both of you take your seats this moment!" Mrs. Howard shuffles to the red button as fast as she can.

Something about Amy, those big brown eyes, intense with confidence, puts a warm glow inside me. I hop up real quick and sorta face Uppercut at an angle, my shoulder grazing his.

"Chill," I tell him. A "bro" or "man" at the end would soften that, but then she might think me and him is tight.

Still staring at her, Uppercut tells me, "Mind. Your. Business."

"You're scared," Amy says. "You're not gonna do anything."

She's got me figured out. Can she hear my heart banging in my chest? But wait—she wasn't talking to me. She's still looking at Uppercut.

He pushes me away and I surprise myself by getting back in the same position. I inch even closer.

"Yes?" It's the secretary's voice over the speaker.

"Please hurry!" Mrs. Howard shouts. "Two students are about to get physical with each other!"

Which is a gift dropped into my hands. "For real?" I ask, looking at each of them. "You two about to *get physical* with each other?"

Laughs all around. Even Uppercut turns his head to show me his busted smile. Nothing from Amy though. She keeps staring down Uppercut for what feels like forever.

"Chickenshit," she finally says, and takes her time walking back to her seat.

For the last few minutes of homeroom I look across the room to Amy again and again. Can't stop checking her out. She's sitting there like the coolest thing ever didn't just happen. I gotta meet this Amy, learn everything about her.

But her interested in a Maesta kid? Even strangers seem to know us. At Florida Palms Mall last weekend me and my boys checked out three cute girls and dared each other to go up to them. After a few rounds of rock, paper, scissors

I walked over all nervous. Even before I opened my mouth the hottest one said, "I don't think so," and the other two laughed more than you'd expect.

Can I fake my way into bravery again? Can I talk to Amy if I pass her alone in the halls? It's gotta be alone. In front of her friends would make me too jittery to talk and in front of my own friends . . . they wouldn't understand.

First-talk scenarios run through my head, good ones like her super thrilled to meet me, her eyes lighting up like some Disney princess. But most of them bad, like her giving me a grossed-out face before hurrying away or laughing like the mall girls.

Then I'm picturing our first date, pizza at DeLucia's in the mall, an outside table, and afterward some hand-holding in a dark movie theater. We a regular perfect-life Kyle and Tina.

Sure, no sweat. I'll just rob a bank first.

How about doing free stuff? We could meet in Brewster Park, go for walks, or just kick it at her place 'cause I'm imagining her parents are cool.

Super cheesy, I know. I'm supposed to be all about hitting it, sex without the love or friendship, but that cheeseball stuff pops into my head all the time. I can't help it.

The thing is, a girlfriend can fix you in a snap. I've seen it. Even short-fuse Kevin who'd swing on anybody over a basketball foul has been chill since Shanice. Guys now call him soft, pussy-whipped for always being with his girl, but all we ever do is talk about girls anyway. Why talk about them when you could *be* with one?

I know loneliness is supposed to be some guy on a desert island, or maybe an old lady knitting and hoping the phone will ring, but loneliness can also be a kid like me, surrounded by tons of people, friends who say "Wassup?" when I see them in the halls or walk through Maesta, friends who kick it with me all the time but only go on about who won the game last night or how some girl's got a sweet ass.

With a girlfriend I wouldn't feel so alone. Maybe Amy, so cool and tough, could be that girl.

2

DURING MY last period I look out the window and see Amy. The school halls are separated by strips of grass, and it's hard to see through some of these hazy old windows, but I spot the back of her head, the blue in her hair, whenever the boy next to her sits up straight or leans back.

"Marcos? May I have your attention, please?"

Ms. J keeps on lecturing about the Constitution, the clock above her head showing two minutes left before my prank starts.

You can feel the charge up in here, the excitement ready to rip through. No offense to Ms. J, who I sorta like. She gets excited about her lessons, talks history like the events happened yesterday.

While other teachers bore themselves as much as us, Ms. J is so into history that she keeps a blog about it. Though I ain't never checked it out, I gotta admit it's cool she has one. On it she supposedly posts reminders of homework, links to videos and websites that can give us more perspective on what we learn in class, so we don't accept just one version of history—that's what she's always saying.

Most of all I like her 'cause last semester she let me do extra credit so I could pass the class. If there's one teacher who should not be pranked, it's Ms. J, but after all those boring classes sometimes I need fun in last period.

These pranks started the first week of school when I came up with a great disruption and gave everybody the instructions. At exactly 2:20 everybody got up, did three jumping jacks, and sat back down.

I remember the screeching of chairs made Ms. J turn from the whiteboard, the last letter going squiggly before she turned to face us. It was the first time I'd seen her frown.

A few weeks later, in the middle of a test, we got up and did a spin while shouting a Michael Jackson *HEE-hee!*

Once we barked.

The week before Christmas we stood, right hands over our hearts, to recite the last line of the Pledge of Allegiance: *With liberty and justice for all.*

I see a girl going into Amy's classroom, probably some office dork with a green slip, which means a family emergency or else you got busted. I know about them slips.

The girl walks over and hands it to Amy. A white slip. I got no idea what they mean.

I check the clock again. Just in time! The thin red

hand's ticking off the last few seconds.

"We have the oldest constitution of any major government," Ms. J's saying, "and it's also—"

We get up, hop onto our chairs, and applaud like our teacher just won *The Voice*. She looks around, maybe trying to spot the kid responsible for this. Her eyes stay on me a little too long.

Her change from shocked to annoyed is always super quick, like when somebody gets pantsed. She's gotta be pushing forty but looks super young right now, waiting with arms crossed, squeezing the blue marker in her right hand. It's the noisiest this class has ever been.

We keep clapping, going on . . . damn! Fifteen seconds! I forgot to tell everybody for how long. Now what? Chloe in the front row whips around first and then everybody's looking at me, the leader. I stop clapping and sit down. They do the same.

Ms. J's also sitting, elbows on her desk, face in her hands.

"Please read Unit 16," she says, so low you can barely hear her. "I need a minute."

The door opens. Mr. Perec from across the hall, shirt pocket holding pens, pokes his torso through the barely opened door. "Everything okay?"

"Yes," Ms. J says.

Not buying that, he comes all the way in to ask us, "What's going on?"

I'd also like the answer to that. Ms. J's hair is a curtain hiding her face. Could she be crying? No way. If the barking prank and Michael Jackson prank didn't break her, this can't have neither. Not in a million years.

"Everything's fine, Mr. Perec," she says, her head still down.

He leaves. The classroom falls quiet except for Ms. J's uneven breathing.

Today's prank kicked ass, but this right now? Not so funny. In fact, it sucks. Ain't gonna feel bad about it though. Don't know why they got teachers in this school who can't take a joke.

Goody-goody Chloe says, "Sorry about the prank, Ms. J. Are you okay?"

"I'm fine." Pronouncing *fine* like it's one word cracked in two. She gets up and hurries outta the classroom, a hand reaching up to touch her hair, sorta blocking her face.

But you can see the tears anyway.

As soon as the door closes Chloe says, "I'm not doing that ever again."

Me neither but why're the girls looking at me? Sure, they was clapping 'cause I told them to, but it's something we all did together.

A few boys smile and shrug, but I don't believe them forced laughs. They feeling bad.

Just like me, I gotta admit.

The office dork walks into our classroom with a handful

of envelopes. That's what Amy musta received instead of a slip. "Hey, where's the teacher?"

She looks at all the desks again, as if Ms. J might be sitting with us.

"We killed her," says Tamara, a girl who might have my detention record beat.

The dork keeps her eyes on the envelope and pronounces slowly. "Mar-cos Rive-ass?"

"Ya gotta be kidding," I say, meaning the pronunciation *and* the envelope.

She walks over and drops it on my desk.

Something for me and for Amy. Could this be a sign?

I tear into it right away. Joe asks me what's inside and a few other kids press around, hovering over my envelope like it's some treasure chest we found together.

I wait for everybody to back off before unfolding the paper inside.

Marcos Rivas:

Congratulations! You've been selected to take part in a new, exciting program. Next Friday, for your sixth-period class, please present this letter to your teacher who will excuse you. Then go promptly to room 212.

Regards,
Principal Jonathon L. Perry

His signature underneath. And I thought *I* had bad penmanship. I peek in the envelope for information on what makes the program exciting, besides Amy being part of it. Nothing in there, but what other sign do I need? Me and Amy got something in common, even if it's only this. Us together ain't crazy. It might be fate.

I try to keep my cool, but inside I'm doing cartwheels.

3

THE NEXT afternoon, I take a deep breath of relief when
I'm outside. I've made it in and outta my house without
trouble from my mom's boyfriend.

Ain't sure I could deal with it today since Amy has
been soaking up all my brain space since, let's see . . . about
thirty-two hours ago, I guess.

I'm taking a second breath, the air nice and fresh in my
lungs, when I see my best friend running this way. Though
Obie moved outta Maesta a few years back he still hangs
around here just about every day.

"Wait!" he says, slowing down and pretending to grab
for the doorknob, his idea of a joke. "Let me say hi to your
boy Hitler right quick."

Easy Obie who never frowns, never says or does a
mean thing, don't take Brian's racism personal like my
other boys who want him dead and wonder why a racist

white guy would live here.

"I know Brian's problem," he says, his hand grabbing again. "He ain't met a brother as charming as me is all."

I shove him away.

If I crack one day and drop the details about my mom's latest boyfriend, Obie will be the guy to hear it. After the first time Brian kicked me for talking back to him I was quieter than usual and Obie said, "Gotta be hard living with him."

I nodded, nothing more, and he didn't mention it again.

He's always been crazy nice like that. When the Frosty's ice cream truck used to roll through, back before the man with the Nestlé cap got jacked and the tinny music was never heard again, Obie'd come up with more coins than me and give me half of the ice cream sandwich. He'd break it the long way, so each of us got some of the chocolate-dipped side.

We used to share toys and candy. Nowadays we share secrets, like how I'm scared of dogs and listen to the Smiths. Or that he pulls straight As and goes to Bible study every Wednesday. Together we've wondered about girls, about kissing and sex, like if it hurts the guys the way it seems to on porn, them goateed faces all twisted up.

So much in common, me and my boy, we even started jacking off at around the same time (though we didn't tell each other about it until a month later—him confessing first and me glad I didn't have to risk being the pervball).

Now I look up at the cloudless sky. With the Florida

sun going down in a pink haze, we got time for one quick game, maybe two. We walk through Maesta, passing two kids on the side of the building practicing goal kicks.

"Any new ideas?" Obie asks.

I shake my head.

With my expenses growing all the time (haircuts, deodorant, acne soap) I gotta get my money right. We fifteen, old enough to work in a few places, but those supermarkets and fast-food joints don't want us. That's why we tried getting into business together two months ago, went door-to-door offering to wash cars. People looked at us like we was carrying a bomb instead of a bucket.

We've also offered to mow lawns, put up Christmas lights, walk dogs, take down Christmas lights, and anything else we can think of. We've tried almost everything except dealing drugs. Obie's too much of a saint for that and I'm too scared. Though doors usually close on our faces, every once in a while a person will look down at our bucketful of clean rags, a bottle of detergent, and a tire brush and ask, "How much?"

Between two sun-bleached cars little Yuri's getting good with the jump rope, the U flipping over her in a green-and-pink flash. She smiles at me and I smile back.

We pass Doña Carmen's place where a TV astrologer is giving predictions in Spanish.

"Wide open," I shout to Obie, my hands up.

When he passes me the imaginary ball, I take an

imaginary jumper, my mind on revenge.

Yesterday, when I went for the shot that shoulda won the game, Art flew up and swatted the ball outta my hands. I'm talking *swat*. They coulda heard it on Mars. And after the ball slammed against the fence, the *oooo* the guys let out was even louder.

I should be getting angry, ready to dominate the court, but I'm still thinking about Amy and fighting the urge to tell Obie about her. Don't know what it is about a crush that makes you want to talk about it. What could I tell Obie? It's not like he ever tells me about Mya, the girl he's been talking to since Christmas vacation. Maybe I should ask him.

"What's up with Mya?"

He shrugs. "Ain't heard from her since Saturday."

Weird. They been spending lots of time lately, mostly sitting on the concrete slab that passes for a porch in Maesta, Mya's mom peeking through the window to make sure there's no touching of lips or hands.

Did he get ghosted? Would Mya do that?

I give Obie an imaginary no-look pass and we keep weaving through the two-floor buildings, following the road that runs through the complex, connecting all the parking lots and Dumpsters.

Taking up a square block of central Tampa, Maesta's a spread of twenty-three look-alike buildings one block south of the train tracks. People who don't know the area, many driving to the famous Teresa's Empanadas, swing a right into here, convinced it's a city road. The man always looks more worried than the woman, and the kids' mouths go round, wide eyes checking out the graffiti on the dust-covered buildings. Though some drivers 180 outta here right away, most cruise around for the other exit.

We pass that broken streetlight where some guy once stood in the dark, pants down, with a view of Art's little sister. Art was too small himself to beat the guy up so he called the cops, who never came.

We pass building E where a Dominican woman lives in apartment four, the one who blasts old-school merengue and lets her kid tricycle around on the court when we in classes. She moved in when Fat Rick got locked up.

With all them people coming and going, we knew what was going down in that place. No other way Fat Rick coulda bought a black Maxima, five years on it, and tricked it out with chrome twenties and that booming Rockford system.

Somebody musta called the cops and that time they *did* roll up, a bunch of them, Tampa Police caps and vests, busting through the flimsy door with guns drawn.

Right now, a red Honda Civic is cruising through, shiny rims spraying sunlight. Our eyes follow as it slows along building G, where Mya lives. Here she comes outta apartment three, looking even hotter than she do at school, wearing a tight sweater and tighter jeans. She hops in and the Honda speeds off, like it's some sorta rescue operation.

That damn near kills me inside, so it's gotta be worse

for Obie. If we was girls, I could maybe say something, but me and my boys don't do emotions.

She went for the guy with decent clothes. And a car instead of a rusty bike.

I say, "Can't believe her mom lets her go out with older boys."

That's me trying to get Obie to focus on the kid's age instead of the money. What else can I say?

Up ahead on the court, Art's going for a corner shot as the others wait under the hoop, legs bent, ready to leap.

It swishes, the net doing a snappy sway. They still warming up.

If there's one dope feature to Maesta, it's the basketball court. Located in the center of this twenty-three-building craziness, it pulls damn near every kid who can dribble a ball. The court, plus the Maesta laundry room, plus the AC our moms yell at us for using, are the reasons why some call this the "luxury projects."

Older kids ball a few blocks away, on the smooth Bridge Baptist Church court. But on this ghetto court you learn to dribble around the holes, and that bent hoop ain't so tricky if you don't shoot off the backboard.

Yesterday's nasty block shouldn't embarrass me none. Art balls better than all of us, even better than most older kids. He's got a wicked dribble, can sink the ball from anywhere, and the air he gets makes you wonder if he's got springs for leg bones.

I figure them ups are from having no seat on his bike. Art's been wanting to earn some money so he could get a seat for the rusty ride his brother gave him, which ain't happened yet. Three years of standing and pedaling muscled his legs so now his fingertips can graze the rim.

After Art swishes another one Obie turns to me. "He's on fire."

"Not for long."

Art's my boy but today he's getting stomped.

We all this way, take games crazy serious. During PE, whether it's volleyball, flag football, or just running laps, Coach Peck tells us winning ain't everything. But Coach Peck don't live in Maesta. Here it's *all* about winning.

As I step on the court the guys eye me, smiling and nodding.

"What's good?" I say. Then to Art, "Payback time, bitch."

He shrugs. We both know who's the best. If I end up on the opposite team and make a shot or steal the ball from him, he smiles like a proud dad at Little League. But today I can beat him. You just gotta need it more.

We taking free throws to see who'll choose up teams when Uppercut points out there's only nine of us.

"Ten." This is from Trey, Art's brother, who plays great for eleven.

He's dressed like Art years ago, light-green hand-me-down sweatpants and sweatshirt stained with red Kool-Aid on the front.

"No way, little man," Ruben says.

Though Ruben's talking about Trey's age, we all wait for the easy comeback.

Trey sucks his teeth. "Who you calling 'little'? Ruben the midget Cuban."

Ruben frowns. His shortness is a sore spot anybody can touch. Go ahead and bust on his clothes, on his curly hair, bust on the fact he came here on a boat made of four truck tires and wooden boards. But call him a midget and watch out.

When he stomps his foot forward and cocks his fist back, Trey flinches with his whole body.

Ruben straightens up. "That's what I thought."

Years back the pronunciation woulda come out *that's what I taught*. His island accent's just about gone but you remember Cuba when he goofs up expressions, or switches word orders like *paper toilet*.

"Yo, Trey," Art says. "Go play with friends." A big bro authority has crept into his voice since their older brother, Cedric, died.

"Gimme my ball then."

Like that's gonna happen. The ball Trey found, totally bald, is our only one since Uppercut punted mine, making it lopsided, after losing a game.

Trey steps back, pissed off, and we shout "Whiteboy!" over and over. Jason's gotta come out when we short a player or else we bang on his door all day. There he is, stepping out and zipping up a hoodie. We got long sleeves today 'cause even though the sun usually burns you up, January in Florida can get cold.

Jason's got this determined hit-man stride, his gray eyes so fierce you half expect him to clock you. I've seen him do that four times, whenever someone dissed him. He ain't with intimidation, that back-and-forth trash talk, just *bam*, a fist to the jaw like when some kid called him "cracker." White kids are supposed to be soft but growing up in a place fifty-fifty black and brown hardened him up something crazy.

When a blue Jeep shows up bumping Taylor Swift, we turn to it like it's a spaceship. Another lost person. A hot white girl to be exact, driving around in what might be her sweet sixteen present. Even with her baseball cap on you can tell she's pretty.

She waves to us and we wave back.

She's totally out of place, like Amy would be if I ever invited her to Maesta. All my life I've seen how couples match, in skin or style, and then I get a crush on a white girl who listens to punk.

"What if someone like her wanted to go out with you?" Damn, I didn't mean to blurt that out.

With Taylor Swift gone, now the guys are all staring at *me*.

Uppercut asks, "Fine as her?"

"White as her."

"Hell yeah, I'd hit that," Art says, and the others agree, some going into detail of what they'd do.

I reword my stupid question. "What if *you* wanted to go out with a girl like that?"

Obie asks, "Who you crushing on?"

"Nobody."

Art says, "The question's why would a girl like that be cool with someone like us? Unless she's a Rachel."

Which bums me out 'cause I know he's right. Rachel who lives here is white the way Jason's white. A technicality.

I yank the ball from Art's hands—"Let's do this"—and stare him down one last time. He nods. He knows it's on.

As the nine players scramble, I stand on the sideline with the ball clutched over my head. Jason jukes out Meatball and is wide open.

The moment I toss the ball, little Trey rushes from the sideline to jump, both hands snatching it from the air, and runs off the court. Soon he's jetting across the parking lot and through buildings K and L.

Some of us give angry looks and words after Trey, while others just curse to themselves, but nobody's trying to catch that kid. We've all tried at one time or another.

4

ME AND my squad are footing it to school, and I can't get there fast enough. After a week of seeing Amy in homeroom and trying to get a look at her during history class, today I'm going to actually talk to her.

I still don't know what the exciting new course will be this Friday, but if I get friendly with Amy before then maybe she'll be happy to find me there. She'll sit next to me, on a seat I will save for her, and that's where our romance will begin.

Days ago, I told myself to be as brave as Amy was with Uppercut and just talk to her, no big deal, but every time I saw her she was with friends or I was with mine.

Not true, Marcos. How about yesterday in the hall, both of us with bathroom passes, nobody else around? My weakass didn't do nothing. When I got close to her, when "hi" or at least a nod woulda been the most normal thing in the world, I turned my head, like the wall suddenly became fascinating.

If there's something that makes you feel more like a dumbass than that, I'd like to know what.

I worry that Amy's too cool for me. The way she stood up to Uppercut proves she's a type of brave that I'm not. But if I'm scared of talking to her, then I prove I'm brave by talking to her, right?

So I gotta do it, can't wuss out. Who cares if she disses me or laughs?

Yeah, right. Who am I kidding? I care. A lot.

We passing the Quickie Pawn, the boarded-up donut shop, and the weedy lot edged with trash when I see my perfect chance to get back at Uppercut. I've been trading punches with him since yesterday. He's two steps ahead, not suspecting nothing when I land a solid fist to the back of his shoulder.

As my boys laugh he turns to give me a big evil grin.

Careful you don't clock Uppercut harder than he do you, else the back-and-forth punching won't stop. Uppercut's the punching champ, hits harder all the time, can make your shoulder go dead for a day.

He's rubbing his shoulder.

"Come on," I say. "That didn't even hurt."

When he nods, I realize I'm screwed.

As we walking along the school field, Obie nudges me in the ribs, which means something's up.

"I gotta take care of something," he says to everybody.

"I'll go with ya," I say, following him onto the grass, toward the baseball field. This is gonna be good. His secrets always are.

Even with the others outta earshot he tells me to hang on, won't say nothing besides "It's in my backpack."

Obie's the only one of us with a backpack. He's got textbooks in there, notebooks and pencils galore. Yep, my best friend's a brain, another thing we don't talk about. Most people don't know, and only a couple guys still call him an Oreo for it.

So nerdy, my boy, that last year he finished second in our class. Got beat by Pia Dhindsa.

And here's another secret: Obie might crush Pia this semester, get a shout-out on the school website with his photo up there and everything, shocking the hell outta them creased-pants dads.

Today Obie seems back to normal after a few days of not saying much and not going out with me to look for work. He mentioned a stomachache on Wednesday and yesterday he said something about an errand with his mom. Suspicious. Maybe he spent two days in his room, extra lonely and sad like I sometimes get.

I see the homeless brown mutt from school, the one the janitor's always feeding. My whole body goes stiff. It's coming straight at us!

Obie claps his hands twice—"Hell outta here!"—which

sends the shaggy thing darting toward the gym. Anybody else would clown me for my fear of dogs, but Obie just keeps them away from me like I'm paying him for it.

Inside of the dingy dugout, he looks both ways before unzipping his backpack.

I see it. "Daaamn."

Two baggies of weed, each the size of a fist. Four nickel bags of crystal meth looking like shiny crushed glass. He sets them on the bench. Eight baggies in total. From a smaller zipper pocket on the side he pulls out two nickel bags full of pink pills.

"Molly?" I ask, taking the tiny bags in my hand.

He nods.

They pale and chalky like them *hug me* and *let's kiss* valentine heart candies, only round.

Why does he have this stuff? His aunt deals, but Obie don't take molly or smoke meth, can't stand weed. One time we smoked a joint and he turned into a paranoid freak for about twenty minutes before conking out.

"It's my aunt's." He starts putting it away.

"Figures."

Obie and I ain't never understood how she moves the stuff. Nearly as wide as the small couch she sits on, that lady don't leave her apartment. Instead of throwing her garbage in the Dumpster, she puts the small bags of trash into bigger bags and leaves them stinking up her porch. She used to give us two dollars to toss it all out but nowadays she hooks us up with two Coors from the fridge, telling Obie, "Not a word to ya mom."

He ain't allowed to visit his aunt, the big-time sinner, though his mom also used to sell, when they lived in Maesta. It's how she came up with the down payment for her run-down house—another secret of Obie's that I been knowing.

He says, "I gave up on other ways of making money, and I ain't trying to rob niggas neither."

"You think I like being broke?"

"Broke is temporary. We poor. And I'm sick of it."

I can't believe this is happening. Dealing? Obie used to call dealing stupid 'cause people always get caught, sooner or later.

People deal until they get caught.

We seen it again and again, last year with Fat Rick and recently, small-time Manrico got busted.

Obie's change of heart must be all about his crush, Mya, riding off with the big-money kid.

Being flat broke cost him a girl. Being poor, I mean.

"You lost your mind?" I ask him.

"Nah," Obie says. "I got it under control. There's no risk."

I look around to make sure we still alone. "You really saying this? *You*? Dealing's always risky."

"But check it out," he says. "I ain't gonna *deal*. It's only *delivering* and nobody finds out 'cause I don't tell nobody."

"Except ya telling me."

"But ya won't talk."

"I know."

"I know too, man. That's why I'm telling ya."

I imagine Obie in juvie over this. What would I do without my best friend, this kid who once punched me in the gut and then apologized for it?

That's how I met Obie, during the summer he moved into Maesta, just before fourth grade. I swiped the Hawks cap off his head and tossed it to Art. A game of keep-away started. Obie ran over to Art who flung the cap back to me. Then Obie stopped right in the middle to talk tough, a general instructing his troops, though he looked only at me. "I ain't doing this forever. Gimme my cap or else." I flung the cap over his head and got hit. A fist to the gut so hard I held the pain with both hands and tipped forward, knees on the pavement.

Obie helped me up and spoke in a tiny voice. "Sorry."

I respected that. The punch and the apology.

We've kicked it every day since, minus his trips to his grandma's, and if I'm straight up, I can tell you that our time together has been the dopest thing in my life.

Now my boy has a backpack full of stuff that could send him to juvie. While I'm happy he'll be making money, and a little jealous that I won't be, I'm mostly worried.

Obie in a juvie uniform looking through bars.

"Careful," I tell him.

The word feels weird in my mouth, and it musta sounded weird too. Obie goes quiet.

Finally he says, "Thanks."

Which also sounds weird. I guess we almost doing emotions, my one word showing I care and his one word showing appreciation. I should probably leave it at that but I gotta do something else.

"Promise?"

I ball my hand and slowly bring it up. This promise fist bump started years ago behind a Dumpster, when we was catching our breath while five kids were chasing us. With whispers and hand gestures Obie explained how we'd go over the fence and through the other lot. To seal the agreement that we'd do it together, never separate even if one of us got caught, we bumped fists without a word.

Now Obie brings up his own fist. "Promise," he says, knuckles pressing against mine.

He explains his new gig, the list of places to hit up after school where he'll collect the paper and hand over the product—an easy hustle.

"And in a few weeks I'll get me them Nikes," he says. "The blue ones with the—"

"I remember which ones," I say, jealous of my own boy.

I spot Amy in the crowd, just a flash of her purple hoodie before she slips down another hall.

I hurry over, super amped, Obie's energy inspiring me

to go for it. I'm feeling better than ever about Amy, a sweet girl no doubt, no reason to be scared. If I get to know her and be nice, she'll be nice back. In my head I even fix the words I'll say. But once I go down the other hall, I feel myself losing heart with every step, becoming weakass Marcos again.

No reason to be scared? I can think of a *million* reasons.

I wanna talk to her but then I see her and hope she hurries away. What's wrong with me?

I lose her in a cluster of kids. No! There she is! Drinking from the fountain, hair in a fist behind her head so it don't get wet. My heart's thumping all wild. I look left and right, like I'm about to cross a street. None of my boys are around.

I wanna be cool, and here's my chance. I wanna be the guy who's brave enough to chat up awesome girls despite the nervy shakes. It ain't just making good on that promise to myself. I really need a girlfriend.

I walk over, my pulse racing, and stop when she straightens up. She turns to me.

I say the only word I can think of at this moment. "Hey."

She wipes her mouth with the back of her hand. "Yeah?" She waits.

"Uh . . . I mean . . . um . . ."

My brain goes blank. I get hot and cold all over. *You stand in front of some super-amazing girl you been crushing on and remember what you wanted to say.*

I gotta freestyle this and make sure I don't sound too ghetto. "I just want you to know that Uppercut's a jerk but I'm not."

"Your friend from homeroom?"

"Antonio, uh-huh, but he ain't really my friend."

She does that I-don't-believe-you head tilt. "So what did your *non*-friend say that day?" All nosy and challenging she asks me, like the Truth or Dare game, both choices in one.

"Can't remember."

She crosses her arms. "Why're you telling me this?"

'Cause I like you. But I don't say that. I ain't stupid.

"'Cause . . . you seem cool. And I want you to know that I'm . . . you know . . ."

"That you're cool too? So we can be cool and chill together? That would be *dope*."

Making fun of how me and my squad talk. Part of me wants to put her in a headlock until she takes it back but the other part of me, most of me, still wants to kiss her.

All around us kids are streaming past, surprise on their faces. The group of girls standing next to room 116 take turns looking at us. Can't blame them. You got a punk girl with blue in her hair and you got me, Maesta Marcos, in my baggy jeans and Jay Z tee.

As long as they don't laugh, we good.

"Yeah, whatever," I say. "Not everybody's like the people they roll with. Just saying."

She uncrosses her arms. "So what did Supercuts say that day?"

No way am I gonna repeat his stupid comment. Not 'cause I'm all about protecting Uppercut. It's her feelings I'm trying to protect. Maybe "skinny crack whore" ain't that mean or even funny but it could make her feel bad, and I ain't having that.

"Can't remember," I say again.

She rolls her eyes. "That's bull."

I try thinking of something smooth to say. Fuck it, I'll just go with what's in my head. "Whatever he says, it's always dumb."

Her hard look softens now. Neither of us say a word. In this magical pause I feel the tiniest chance of something between us.

"If he's not your friend, how come you hang out with him?" Suddenly her deep-brown eyes bug at something behind me.

I whip around.

Uppercut smiles. "Wassup, Marcos?" and slams a fist into my chest. It knocks all the air outta my lungs and hurts like hell. I'm slumped over and wheezing. Worse than that, Amy's watching, mouth hung open.

When Uppercut walks away laughing, she takes a step toward me. "You okay?"

I might be dying. Is this how I'm going out? Suffocating from a payback punch in the main hallway while kids with backpacks watch? Dead at fifteen?

Amy, it coulda been the greatest love this century, but now we'll never know 'cause you standing here asking me a question instead of calling 9-1-1. I need an ambulance, or maybe just the school nurse.

"Dude?" Amy steps closer. "Are you okay?"

I try to answer yes but nothing comes out.

I'm bent over, hands on my knees to keep me from tipping. Focusing on my breathing, it gets better, little by little, though inhaling still hurts.

I stand up straight. "Okay, sorry. I'm good now. Where were we? What was I saying?"

Amy's mouth is still open. "What's wrong with you people?"

You people? Is this girl a damn racist? Maybe she's one of them neo-Nazis I've seen on TV who sorta got a punk look going. The guys shave their heads but maybe the girls don't gotta.

"Us people?" I ask her.

"Boys are violent idiots," she says, and takes off, lost in a swarm of kids.

5

ON THURSDAY, a day before my special new class with Amy, they got me in the office. Principal Perry studies the computer screen, steady scrolling the mouse, all them details telling him who I am.

This must be about what went down in the cafeteria today, and I ain't trying to get suspended. Don't get me wrong. If the suspensions ain't too many, if they don't mean I gotta redo the school year, they like mini-vacations that give me time to work on my game. Sometimes it's dope to be alone, the court as blank as an after-school whiteboard, the sound of bouncing caused by my hands only, the hush of the ball arcing through the sunshine, toward the hoop.

But I ain't got no ball and right now suspension would mean hanging out at home with my mom's boyfriend. Worst of all, if I'm home with Dipshit Deluxe it means I ain't at the new exciting class with Amy tomorrow, chatting her up, saying funny and suave things to win her over.

That class is my chance to be with Amy, to show her that we got something in common.

This here office is pretty sweet. Ain't gonna lie. The last pervy principal had this place set up nice, and the new principal ain't redecorated. Same shiny wooden desk and black leather throne, same beige blinds blocking out most of the sun, some degrees and certificates walling the office, and under them, still swimming like champs, the same colorful fish.

I've been into fish ever since the field trip to the Florida Aquarium, where the slogan's "Inches from Amazing."

It really *was* amazing, all those lives in that huge tank, though everybody else was sneaking looks at their phones. I wanted to get closer to the fish, swim with them, even with the slow-flapping stingrays and the sharks wiggling by that coulda messed me up something serious. It's different seeing something up close instead of on a screen. Maybe all living things are amazing if you get close enough to really look.

At one corner of the fish tank a filter's spurting tiny bubbles that the red round fish in the opposite corner has gotta be afraid of. I ain't seen him move yet.

What if the other fish are cool with life in the tank? It ain't *totally* crazy. They don't know oceans from elbows, know nothing about a water wonderland thousands of miles wide, where they could endlessly explore. Best of all, here they got each other, ain't gotta worry about looking for food or becoming it.

Last semester I counted fifteen and now there's fourteen. The poor little guy, lollipop red, is sulking in the corner as the other thirteen coast back and forth.

And what's taking Perry so long? The last principal got both sides of the story, chose a version to believe, and sentenced you—detention or suspension. While I used to hope he'd give me my punishment in a hurry and not lecture my ears off, a part of me also hoped he'd try chatting me up. I know that makes no sense.

Perry now raises his eyes to me. Guy's got the worst comb-over I ever seen. "Your last semester of sophomore year and you couldn't go two weeks without visiting me."

If he wants a response, he better ask me a question. I'm wondering if I can get outta this. Though Principal Pervert gave out punishments automatically (Small fight? Five days detention. Bloody fight? Two days suspension), this new guy could be different. Maybe I can sorry-up my voice and get outta a punishment.

Perry tells me he knows what happened, that the music teacher, cafeteria cop for today, saw the whole thing with Zach.

"Help me understand why you were going to fight."

"I wasn't gonna fight." Like it's the craziest idea ever. "I just pushed him a little."

"And why did you push Zach?"

"He spilled milk on me." I point to my left sleeve, dry now, but don't actually touch my shoulder. The bruise my mom's boyfriend gave me for leaving a plate unwashed still hurts.

"Spilled, that's correct. He said it was a mistake." Perry's big rumbling voice fills the office so completely it's a miracle my own fits. "Zach didn't actually *pour* the milk on you, did he?"

"He coulda said sorry." I go for calm, figure that might help, but the words come out wrong.

Perry don't blink. "Perhaps you didn't give him the opportunity to apologize."

I shrug.

Here's the thing: when I felt the whiteboy's foot trip on my chair leg, I turned to watch the open carton of milk slide down the tray and flip on the edge. I tried dodging it but the milk splashed cold on my shoulder before hitting the floor.

Getting hit with the milk made me angry and sorta happy at the same time. Can't explain why. Go ahead, twist my arm. All I know's I hopped up right away to shove Zach's punkass on the floor.

Since sixth grade when we had the same teacher, I've sorta known Zach, the skinny front-row kid with all the right answers. How dope to see him on the cafeteria floor today, his panicky eyes looking up at me. Everybody around me sprung up, my boys and the rest of the free-lunch crew shouting for me to clock Zach. Tonya told me to leave the poor whiteboy alone, but the other girls wanted a fight as much as anybody. Soon the whole cafeteria was standing. Mr. Giles stepped into duty, snaking through the crowd, an action hero in a brown polo shirt. Obie grabbed me and we took off with the rest of our boys.

But now I'm in the office.

Perry crosses one leg over the other. "So what would your parents say about this?"

"No parents. Just my mom."

"Okay, Marcos." He must think parents and a mom are the same thing. "What would your *mother* say about this?"

"She wouldn't care."

A half smile, like I told him my nuts are solid gold. "She wouldn't care?"

So that wasn't a real question. It was one of them tricks to get you to say what grown-ups *think* they already know.

"She wouldn't care, sir," I say.

Here's a fun test: tell people your dad's an asshole 'cause he ain't around, or 'cause he beats you with a tire iron. You'll get a *that's-life* shrug. But tell them your mom ain't exactly the greatest person who ever lived and they don't believe you.

Perry stares me down with the same eyes Uppercut uses to pick out wusses in the halls. Is he looking for fear? My fear?

He uncrosses his legs and picks up the phone. "We'll see about that."

He dials and asks for my mom, Maria Rivas, pronouncing it right. I sit listening to the bubbling-hum of the tank filter and watch the fish.

My mom works a checkout lane at Walmart. I imagine a manager walking up to her now as she waves items through the beeping laser bars, another blue-vested lady taking over.

"Yes, Ms. Rivas? This is Principal Perry from Hanna High. I am here with your son . . . You see, he almost got into a fist fight . . . Ms. Rivas? . . . I thought you would like to know . . . Well, I am not sure what we are going to do with him . . . No, there is nothing else. Have a nice day."

He hangs up and sighs. The weird smile's gone.

"I'd like to know something, Marcos." A squeak escapes the throne when he leans back. "Are you going to give me any more trouble this semester?"

I'm giving *him* trouble? Sorta like two summers ago when I got busted swiping a Snickers from Walgreens. I waited in the back of the squad car until my mom showed up to sweet-talk the mall cop. After it got sorted out, walking from the cop car to her car, the first thing outta her mouth was "How embarrassing." The second thing, after the car finally cranked, was "How could you do this to me?"

But I didn't do nothing to her. I did it to the Snickers.

I'm looking down at the gray carpet now. "I won't give you no trouble, sir." Am I overdoing it? I keep my head down, focus on the hole in my sneaker.

"I've reviewed your record, Marcos, so you have to reassure me somehow."

I check out the tank again—a shot of red in there. The round fish has started swimming! It's finning around pretty damn fast.

"I'm talking to you, Marcos. What is going on with you?"

Is he talking about this moment or always? Do I explain why I'm into fish, or tell him my life sucks? Not that I'd go into nothing private.

And besides, you see any Hollywood cameras around? This ain't no cheeseball movie with the super-caring white person who shows up, does good, and *abracadabra*, life's a basket of rainbows. Principals and teachers don't give a damn. They just want you to sit still and shut up.

I'm a few feet from amazing but I walk over to get closer. I see my reflection in the glass.

"Sit down, Marcos."

Man, that chubby red fish would take off for miles if it could. Sucks that he's gotta swim back and forth forever.

"Marcos?"

I turn to Perry. "Who takes care of these fish?"

"What?" It's like he's seeing the tank for the first time. "Who's in charge of them?"

"I'm not concerned with the fish right now."

"I guess you feed them since they're in your office and all, but they've always been here. Who do they belong to?"

"Marcos." His eyebrows are almost touching each other.

Even after answering all their questions, you try asking a simple one and they act like you just farted on their lunch.

I look at the miniature lives again. I can picture both principals sprinkling the flakes over the water, then sitting back down, not bothering to watch the tiny fish mouths sucking in their food with a kiss and a slurp. I can also picture Juan the janitor feeding them on Saturday when school opens for detention, but nobody's here on Sundays.

"Somebody feed them on Sundays?"

"Don't concern yourself with the fish," he says, getting more annoyed. "You should be concerned with yourself right now."

I stop myself from rolling my eyes and go sit down. He don't wanna say "I don't know." Grown-ups can't say them three words in a row. And he don't care if the fish eat on Sundays while he probably eats a great buffet breakfast and then lunch and dinner too.

"So tell me, Marcos. Do you have anything to say for yourself?"

I picture my mom's boyfriend sitting on the armchair

all day. Amy in that class without me. "I'm sorry. It won't happen again."

When Perry leans back I can't tell if he's nodding or if the throne's rocking him a bit. "I'm going to let you off the hook this one time, so you can attend your course tomorrow."

"Thanks."

"You are skating on thin ice, Marcos. One more bad move and I will suspend you and drop you from the course. I'll be watching you."

"I can go?"

I wait as he turns to the computer and types.

"You are already ten minutes late for class," he says, "so I won't keep you any longer."

I thank him and leave. I got away with it, something the last principal wouldn't let me do. As I head to class I'm feeling pretty good until I remember the other problem.

My mom might tell her boyfriend about this.

6

WITH EVERY step home my bones are getting shakier.

I turn the knob and softly push the door so the hinges don't squeak. Brian faces me anyway, squinty eyes sucking the life outta me.

I've tried a bunch of greetings—*Hi, Hello, Hey*—and in different ways, sometimes dropping his name at the end. He gives me either a grunt or a nod. Once I didn't say squat and he told me to learn some damn manners. Yesterday I gave "Good morning" a shot and he called me a faggot. From now on I'm keeping it simple.

Check him out on the armchair, the goofy bastard— long legs spread open, dumb face and bushy mustache. A *Nifty at Fifty* koozie keeping his beer cold though he ain't even forty. Since getting fired he mopes around mornings and afternoons too. Only the beer's different, switched from Bud to nasty Natural Ice.

"Hi," I say in a low voice.

An annoyed grunt and he's looking at me again. Staring. When my mom's around, her eyes can roam the room without ever landing on me.

If Brian found out what went down at school he must be saving it for later.

He moved in last summer, just before the worst heat wave in a decade, but the strangling humidity didn't faze him none. The douche sat in the armchair (my armchair when my mom's between boyfriends) with the fan pointed at himself. Even with me and my mom also watching TV, even though the fan has an oscillating setting, it forever pointed his way.

Now I'm just trying to fill up on some grub and head to the court. I'm about to pass Brian when I hear that raspy voice. "Marcos." No choice but to stop.

"I looked out the window just now," he says.

Typical Brian comment, outta nowhere, and the smile tips me off that more's coming.

He don't always mess with me. It's a straight-up coin toss when I leave my room or come home, so it's better to keep my mind on something else. I like to think about myself crushing on the basketball court.

"Saw you with that nigger," he says. "You getting any?" Big smiles always make his brown mustache stretch straight.

"Desiree's a neighbor," I say, and start for the kitchen again.

Nowadays, Brian's got more time to think up ways to come at me. Seven weeks it's been since him and another worker fought during some landscaping job, an actual fist-fight in a Clearwater condo complex. Despite his busted lip, a sight that cheered me up for days, Brian swore up and down he won.

"Not bad for a nigger," he says now. "You should get some."

"Spics" and "niggers" is what he calls us, in a way that makes you think of Confederate flags and burning crosses. He always popping off at the mouth about how niggers don't work and how spics steal all the jobs. We supposed to be the scummiest of the earth's scum, but I guess he makes an exception for my mom.

I feel my stomach grumble. When I escaped the cafeteria today, I left almost half my free lunch uneaten. I'll fix me a quick grape jam 'cause my boys will be waiting for me on the court.

"You need to get along with Brian," my mom used to say. Right. Like I love getting harassed. Even after hearing how he talks she still kept saying that. Finally I caught on—that I better annoy him less. I do that by staying outta the house.

I was crazy cool with Brian in the beginning. How can you not like a guy who brings over a huge pizza loaded with toppings? We all sat at the table where he cracked some jokes, made my mom sorta smile and talk, which had me wishing he lived here.

Careful what you wish for. Ain't that what they say? A week later Brian did move in, brought two duct-taped boxes and a Hefty bag full of clothes. That's how it happens with boyfriends, in a snap. It's *Hi, nice to meet you* and one morning, a week or two later, the guy's sitting in front of the TV in underwear, sometimes a shirt too, if I'm lucky.

I didn't mind with funny, pizza-bringing Brian. Plus he always wears pants.

Nights we watched TV together. He explained the eighties references of *Family Guy*, let me be the boss of the remote, shared his food—chips, cookies, even a piece of his steak once. Walking into our living room you woulda thought we was a happy family, perfect except that Pops was the wrong color.

My mom's boyfriends always made me feel like an overstaying visitor, but with Brian, at first, it wasn't that way at all. For a few weeks home was an okay place to be.

"I'm serious." His voice is louder. "Why don't you get some from that nigger?"

I got two words for him—*fuck you*—but say them only inside my brain. I tell him, "*You* get some."

That sorta back talk, a few hours and many beers later, would get Brian all up in my face, my heart machine-gunning in my chest.

With no time for grape jam, I shove the last flimsy

piece of Great Value bread in my pocket and fill a glass from the tap.

"Don't worry about me, dipshit," I hear. "I get your mom's pussy every night."

I choke on a gulp and set down the glass. Even with the TV cranked and my coughing, Brian's laugh drifts over. Sticks and stones, I remind myself, heat rushing through me.

I imagine bashing his head with the table lamp until he stops moving. Wonder how many hits it would take. One day I'll stomp him good, with just fists. Sure, I'm twig-skinny but my daily push-ups are up to thirty, and changes can happen super quick.

It's true I do stupid stuff sometimes, burn my toast or forget to zip my fly, but hearing "dipshit" has my back teeth grinding so hard they hurt. Plus that comment about . . .

Calm down, Marcos, I tell myself.

I unclench my fists and take a deep breath.

Again I wonder if this Brian is the same Brian I first met. Am I so dumb that the pizza and jokes distracted me? You know, like how a pretty girl can make you tune out that she's dumber than a stick and sorta mean? Anyway, this Brian's the only one here now, and I've gotten plenty used to him.

Things can switch from weird to everyday business. Like after two weeks of the neighbors fighting I could fall asleep despite the man's angry words and the lady's screams, the hitting, all of it seeping through, humming through my bedroom wall.

Same with Brian. After a few weeks of "Hey, dipshit" and "spic" it became normal. When the hating gets worse and comes at you more often, you get used to that too. Maybe you can get used to anything.

I used to pretend me and Brian was tight so my mom wouldn't pick up on nothing. Crazy, huh? Like I was ashamed (though I did nothing wrong), or like I was his accomplice (though nothing was in it for me).

Not that snitching would help. My mom saw the top of my arm that one time, spotted the bluish-green bruise when I reached for my SpongeBob cereal bowl one morning. She actually looked worried.

I admitted to eating one of his chocolate chip cookies. How was I supposed to know he counted them? My mom sucked her teeth and shook her head. Then she grabbed her margarine tub filled with rice and beans and took off for work.

I guess some kids might call the cops, but snitching ain't me. That's admitting you ain't tough or can't handle life.

Now I down the rest of my glass, wash it, dry it, and put it back in the cupboard. That's Brian's rule. He leaves dirty dishes in the sink, in the living room, the nasty ashtray on the windowsill, empty beer cans beside the armchair, his shirts everywhere. Me, I gotta be crazy neat and clean for all of us like some sorta ghetto butler.

Here I go, doing my ghostly creeping from the kitchen to my room for my basketball clothes. Looks like he didn't find out about my trouble at school. It's just a regular in-and-out mission today. But as I head down the hallway I hear him ask, "You getting any pussy at all?"

"Tons," I say, hoping for a laugh.

I hope for a lot when it comes to Brian. Especially when he does things that can pass for nice, which confuses the hell outta me. One time he drove me to Saturday morning detention so I wouldn't have to walk in the rain, and on Christmas he gave me his old no-credit phone.

I click my bedroom door closed behind me, the sound calming me a little. This room's home, the only place Brian don't hang out though sometimes he barges in. Inside these four tight walls is where I listen to my hip-hop, soul, and also the Smiths. I love how Morrissey sings about whatever he wants, even admits to writing in a diary.

I turn the radio on for a few seconds while I change into my raggedy shorts. It's that new joint by Drake, another guy who can sorta get away with showing emotions.

Though you don't choose what plays on the radio, when life sucks extra bad and you feel lonely, you can switch it on and know that a bunch of people, maybe thousands, are listening to the same song or commercial as you, at the exact same time. It can chill you out some.

I take a big bite outta the slice of bread and chew

quickly. When I'm on the last mouthful I hear him call me: "Dipshit!"

I swallow it down and open the door. "Yeah?"

"*I* used to get tons," he says. "But nothing compares to your mom's snatch."

I go pick up the first thing, the ceramic Virgen de la Divina Providencia on my dresser, mine since my grandma died—*No, I can't break this*—and set it back down. I take a deep breath and count, but soon lose track of the numbers. Don't know how my legs move. All I know is I'm standing here in the middle of the living room, behind Brian, the blood in my arms oozing down, curling my hands into fists.

Brian turns to me, smiling like I brought him a gift. "Looks like you're about to do something."

What if it ain't too late? Maybe I can save myself! I ain't said nothing yet and the fists disappear if I open my hands, right? Then I can join my boys on the court. Except I can't unclench my fists for some reason. And though fear has kept me zipped quiet for months, right now I'm even more afraid of not speaking. Every time I force my mouth shut when it wants to open, a little piece of me chips away.

Brian gets up and walks over. His silence, his stillness . . . Trust me, it's scarier than anything. I swallow the lump in my throat, and though my arms tremble, I stare him down. I ain't gonna let myself disappear completely.

"You a drunk, white trash, no-job-having . . ."

I take just one step back before his hands grab my tee.

Then I'm up, the air whooshing under me. My back slams on the floor. I feel it right down to my toes. Brian sits on me so hard my ribs might snap.

"Think you can take me?"

His knees are pinning my arms down. His hand squeezing my throat. I can't breathe.

"I'll take you *and* your faggot friends. Used to take on ten guys at a time."

Dissing him's the dumbest thing I've ever done! He's gonna kill me. I decide to yell, someone in Maesta will hear me, but a squeaky whisper comes out. When I twist my body some air sneaks into my lungs. Brian grips tighter, his thumb digging into my neck.

A TV joke fills the room with fake laughter.

All of a sudden the door opens. "What? Hey! What's going on?"

Brian's hand lets go and my lungs pull in a bunch of oxygen. Breathing ain't easy. The exhaling happens quickly but the inhaling takes work. You gotta focus on sucking in more air, holding on to it, getting the breathing rhythm right.

My mom's in the doorway, keys in one hand, her blue Walmart vest in the other. She don't move toward us, don't budge at all. Just watches me and Brian with big eyes. My mom's actually looking at me.

Brian says, "This little shit thinks he can disrespect me."

When I wriggle an arm loose Brian jams it back under his knee. His wide shoulders tip forward, and though I can breathe now this might be worse. Muscle's grinding against bone. I'm fighting back the tears. Instead I flex my biceps, which makes them hurt more.

Brian crosses his arms and smiles. I know what he wants. I've given it to him five times before.

"Come on, Brian," my mom says, like he's running late for a job interview.

Does she think that's good enough to work? Brian tips forward again, the grinding in my arms going deeper. When I squeeze shut my eyes, a tear slides down and settles in my ear.

"Brian?" My mom's voice softer now. "Come on."

The pain's too much.

"Okay!" I blurt out. "Sorry! I didn't mean it!"

Another smile and he shifts his weight back. "Not as tough as you think, huh, dipshit?"

He gets on his feet and yanks me up by the shirt, my arms still burning. Brian sits on the armchair to watch his show again, legs spread open.

When my mom's eyes lower, I also notice it—my tee ripped in two places. The circle of the collar and some of the sleeve have separated from the rest. The new black tee I got for Christmas.

My mom sees her present hanging on me, a rag in three pieces, and still she's standing there, a total statue. Don't know about you, but to me if you live with someone, and especially if that someone's your mom, she should talk. And if not on the daily then that person should talk now, to the cops on the phone or tell Brian to get the hell outta our house.

Don't think I ain't noticed how my friend's moms are— the questions and speeches, the round-the-clock worry.

I realized how messed up my mom is at Art's twelve-year-old birthday party. The brokest of us all, with two brothers and a little sister, Art got no present other than a chocolate cake with no icing. But I felt jealous of him anyway. The singing did it.

Me and my boys, too cool to sing, just mouthed the words of the happy birthday song. But Art's family sang loud enough for all of us, sang like they really meant it, like they wanted him to be happy not only that day but every day of the year and for the rest of his life. It was the nicest thing you ever heard, and I ain't talking about their voices. They'd get booed off any talent show stage.

My mom never sings shit. And for my birthday, which lands at the end of summer, she gives me some back-to-school supplies and says "Happy birthday" the same way she says "The beans are ready."

All my life I've hoped that she had some love for me under her coldness, and that any day she'd bust it out like a family heirloom she was saving for the right time. Now's the moment for that.

My mom closes the front door all quiet and careful, then slowly hangs the keys on the wooden elephant on the wall. Like they're the two most delicate tasks ever.

She waits. You'd swear I was blocking her way or something.

My heart's no longer banging and I'm watching her, my so-called mom, thin and nervous beside the front door. I feel love for her now. Especially now. A love so pathetic I should probably walk away in shame but something's rooting me here until I figure out, once and for all, what she's about.

I know there ain't no guarantee that a person you love will give a damn about you, and I know I shouldn't be tearing up like some little bitch, but I wanna know something. What am I supposed to do with this love I got? 'Cause even though her favorite words are *Leave me alone*, and even though she prefers her asshole boyfriend to me, I can't unlove her no matter how much I try.

I look at my mom. With that curly hair pulled back, face in full view, I see myself in her—the tan skin, the mud-colored sadness living in the eyes. The one photo of my dad got tossed away years ago but it don't matter. I'm my mom's kid all the way.

Right now she looks about sixteen, the age she was when she got pregnant. I'm trying to see a mom in front of me, but that right there's just a girl.

Brian asks, "What the hell ya looking at?"

My mom's miles and miles away. So far that we might as well be on different planets.

"Don't know," I say, and I leave for the courts.

7

I RECOGNIZE some of the faces at the mystery course. Here are the kids who slump in the back rows, the ones the last principal knew by name. Only ten of us in here so far, though the bell just rang. Amy ain't around, dammit. I had it all worked out: I'd walk in tardy, hurry to find a random seat, and *whoops*, discover Amy next to me.

What a dump! A reject classroom for reject kids. A whiteboard stained yellowish in some spots. Instead of the regular one-person desks it's tables for two students, the tops tagged and doodled.

Just like the first day of school, everybody's small in their chairs, no eye contact or talking. With the back row full I go for the empty table in the middle. I walk over with my poker face on and slide into it. All day I've been wearing this face to show everyone how normal I am. Definitely not sad from yesterday.

FRED ACEVES

I take another look around the classroom, half-expecting cops to bust in and arrest everybody.

Zach shows up, the kid I shoved in the cafeteria yesterday. Just my luck. I don't wanna look at him for some reason. Zach, the skinny front-row kid with the right answers. What's he doing here with *us*?

He's rocking a suit jacket, black corduroy over jeans, and sneakers. That's his style, sorta old-school and classy. Must be a thrift-shopper. He slows down for a second when he sees me, then takes a seat in the front.

I don't wanna kick his ass. That's so forgotten I ain't even angry no more.

I'm remembering back in sixth grade when he answered questions right and our teacher said, "Very good, Zach!" She said that about a million times a day.

During recess most kids played baby games—four square, hopscotch, tetherball—while some of the boys, like my squad, like Zach, played basketball. He balled good, I gotta admit. Whenever he scored on me I'd say "Very good, Zach!" in the teacher's voice and everybody peed themselves laughing.

What a mean switcheroo, turning a little victory for him into shame. Now I'm feeling shame, remembering how he looked on the cafeteria floor.

Shoving him is something Uppercut would do. Brian too. That thought chills me to the bone.

Amy comes in with her bored walk, chewing gum like

rules can't mess with her. After recognizing me, her eyes slide away. When she's near enough, a crazy impulse gives me guts.

"Hi."

The other kids are looking at me, but she's gonna keep walking, a total dis. Is that so bad? But no! It's gonna be way worse! She's gonna make a scene. Gonna do me like she did Uppercut.

"Hi," she says back.

Yes! Though she don't smile, and it's the quickest *hi* ever, I count it as a win.

Only one problem. After meeting my eyes she looked at the thumb-shaped hot sauce stain just under my white collar. I tried to get it out with bleach but the red stain just turned bright yellow.

I'm forever worried about how poor I look. My clothes I get from Walmart, a few sizes big so they last. As an employee my mom has dibs on the discounted stuff. Jeans I got in the eighth grade now fit me right. But big clothes on a smaller body's okay, sorta the hip-hop fashion, maybe started by no-money moms. Only the tube socks fit snug on day one, though weeks later the elastic gives up and pools around the ankles.

Amy goes for the table in the second row with her rocker friend, a fat kid who wears a different metal band tee every day. Though he's too dorky to consider competition, they could sorta make sense in ways that me and Amy couldn't. Sure, he's about metal and she's about punk, but it's all rock music.

Times like this make me hear "dipshit" in Brian's voice, and I guess I *am* stupid. But if I get shocked by my own stupidity there's a smart part of me noticing it, right? So I ain't *completely* stupid.

Everybody's staring straight ahead, each latecomer more awkward than the last as they decide between the last few seats. You'd swear we didn't all sorta know each other from other classes. In the staff lounge the teachers probably say hi to each other, at least, but 'cause we students, the opposite of teachers, I guess we gotta do the opposite.

"Dude, there's exactly two girls here." This from Pete in the back who never shuts up. In detention it gets him an extra day.

He's right though. Lots of guys and two girls, Amy by the window and another girl in the front row, short and tucked into her seat so I can only see the pink headphones clamping her curly red hair.

Amy turns to face the loudmouth. "Pete? Exactly zero people give a shit."

As a response, he burps her name out—"Aaaaaay–MEEEEEEE!"—really stretching out both syllables.

A man in squarish glasses comes in shouldering a backpack, a simple gray JansSport some kids also haul around. Most teachers carry these soft briefcases with long shoulder straps. He sets it on the desk and introduces himself as Mr. Breckner. The girl up front takes off her headphones.

"Welcome to Future Success, a program that will help put you on the right track."

How's this guy know which track we on? *He's* definitely on the wrong track with them goofy clothes, a green tee with *Future Success* across the chest that's tucked into grandpa jeans. He chills for a few beats before pacing again.

"All of you were chosen by teachers as smart students with tremendous potential. However, you're not doing well academically."

Smart? Which teacher considers me that? I run through the list in my head, from first-period English to Ms. J for history and everybody in between. I can't imagine who it was. In algebra, Mr. Santos has noticed me doing equations without writing them down. Is that smart? And I remember for English I got me an A plus for the first essay we had in class—*How I Spent My Summer*—but that's just writing about what happened, not smart.

It feels good knowing a grown-up believes in me, that stupidity don't explain my bad grades. I know I can do better. And if I put in the work like Obie, maybe I can do great.

I take my hundredth glance at Amy and the rest of my thoughts turn off. Even slouching, boredom on her face, she's the most beautiful girl in the world. You might say *yeah, right,* and of course she's only got a 4.2 on that mean

Rate Your Classmates site, but this crush is doing something so black-magicky on me I wouldn't trade her for a rap video girl.

Now I'm learning that this girl's beauty, guts, *and* brains.

Breckner asks, "What is keeping you from reaching your academic potential?"

I wait for the answer.

"The right tools," he says. "Knowing how to take notes, how to prioritize homework, how to study for tests, and much more. This course will give you the tools you need to improve your grades."

Maybe I need tools. I need *something*. The first two weeks of this semester I ain't done homework or read a single page in my textbooks. It's always the same with me. I do squat for months and then spend the last few weeks playing catch-up.

Bad grades is what I got in common with Amy and everybody else here.

Still pacing, Mr. Breckner says, "We are to meet here every Friday for your last-period class, and stay for an extra half hour, unless you have a bus pass."

Everybody groans but me. Ninety minutes every week with Amy? For the rest of the school year? News don't get better than this. Right here, in this Future Whatever club, things will be different between us. We'll talk, get to know each other. She'll forget that day with Uppercut, forget I even know him. She'll see me for me, Marcos without the Maesta, and catch on that maybe it can be me and her forever.

After the school bell rings and the other classes empty, Breckner keeps talking about how he'll be tracking our progress, with the help of our teachers and our study journals. He says we'll have fun every week and even go on a field trip in the middle of the semester.

When he dismisses us, Amy takes off with the metalhead kid. It crushes me inside, knowing that I got the whole weekend before seeing her again, and probably another week until I can talk to her.

Without my boys around, I gotta do my detention day walk, a lonely twenty blocks home. Just as I'm coming up on the gas station I get this weird feeling, a worry that hits me all at once. I turn my head and see Zach half a block behind me.

I pretend I don't see him and keep walking like I'm scared. It hits me that I am scared. Not of Zach but of what's in my head. I can't stop thinking about how I shoved him yesterday.

When did I become Uppercut? The thought's so awful that I wanna hurry down the sidewalk, but I don't. I'm not about to run away from who I am.

I stop and turn back. As I'm walking toward Zach he looks around, as if for a hiding place. To his right, a guy at the pump filling his truck. To his left, across the street, the

Ely's Discount parking lot. He stops cold and tenses up.

Then I stop, not exactly calm either. "Hey."

"Hey," he says in a low voice.

Not knowing what else to say, I come up with "Saw you in Future Success class."

He nods.

So much for my brilliant small talk. I should just come out with it. "That whole cafeteria thing yesterday? I'm sorry about that."

Another nod. "Okay."

With nothing else to say we start walking.

"Weird class, huh?" he says.

"Very weird."

We talk about the study journals Breckner wants us to keep. Then Zach mentions the funny way Breckner paces and how he talks way too much. After a while it don't feel strange hanging with Zach. It's like the new kid on the block that you've seen around has finally spoken, and you know he'll be a friend soon.

He asks, "Did you notice his jeans?"

I tuck in my shirt and hike up my jeans. With Zach laughing I take a few steps like that. Across the street, a man's coming outta the bakery with a huge loaf of bread.

I shout to him, "If we wanna succeed, we need the tools to succeed!"

The man does a look-around, cap pointing every which

way. Then he shakes his head before climbing into his Ford F-150.

Zach's impression beats mine no contest, especially the way Breckner says, "Okay, people?" He nails the voice and the way Breckner bunches his lips, adjusts his glasses while thinking.

"Hmmm." Zach tilts his head and puckers his lips to one side. "Did I poop yesterday?" His face relaxes. "I believe I did. Okay, people, let's study so we can succeed!"

We laughing hard. You'd think that cafeteria shove happened centuries ago. When I'm more than halfway home, curiosity gets me. "You live out this way?"

"Sorta. For now. I don't know." The front-row kid with all the right answers stumped by my simple question.

At some point he had the *tools* to succeed and he probably didn't lose them. Maybe something else messed him up.

Zach kicks a rock and it does a quick roll before leaping into the street. I guess he don't wanna answer me, which makes me wanna know even more.

"I'm sorta living with my grandma," he finally says. "My mom's got cancer."

I stand still from the shock. He stops walking a couple of steps ahead. He ain't playing.

Zach's stylish haircut and white skin and freckles. It's crazy. You should be able to look at people and know they got it rough.

69

"The chemo worked but then, like, it didn't or whatever." He's looking down like it's his fault. "She doesn't have much time left."

"Holy fuck."

Life can suck in different ways for different people. Something I know but that just got realer with Zach in front of me. His eyes shine with the start of tears. I keep walking so he don't see me see him cry.

Besides, even if I wanted to talk, where would I find the words?

8

AFTER LUGGING the bucket through new neighborhoods Saturday by myself, offering to wash cars and getting nos, I got so down that on Sunday I just stuck around my hood trying not to worry about money. It's worse when you need a haircut. Even if you can keep your hand from reaching up and feeling the top of your head, and even if you avoid mirrors, you'll always have a friend to point it out.

In my case I got four boys talking trash about my wild hair all weekend.

I'm $5.36 away from a haircut at Benny's Barbershop, the cheapest place I know. I'm trying to look my best for Amy this Friday, and if I can't get a new wardrobe then at least I can tame this mini-fro that's starting to cover my ears.

Okay, so I didn't talk to Amy after Future Success, but at least I said hi to her and she said hi back. Next time I'll say more, talk to her like a friend, just like I did with Zach.

Best of all, I'll do it with a fresh new haircut and a new shirt, thanks to a brilliant idea I got.

Last night me and Art was talking about Obie's new Nikes, the blue Hyperdunks with the silver speckles. Art got jealous and angry at being poor, couldn't believe Obie's making that kinda money helping his aunt clean houses. (That's the lie me and Obie are sticking to.)

Since turning sixteen, Art's been hitting up even more places that hire at that age. Art's a year older than us, by the way, got held back in junior high for skipping. In the last three months he's filled out a million applications but ain't had a call yet.

I got to thinking why and had a lightbulb moment. With all them applications managers receive, the job experience section blank, I figured Art needed to stand out somehow. So I convinced him to meet the managers, shake their hands, so he ain't some random kid.

And walking to school this morning I got another smart idea when we passed the Amscot shopping plaza. A strong wind sent an empty pretzel bag cartwheeling through the parking lot before it slid across the sidewalk and onto the street. There was more litter, mostly empty wrappers and plastic bottles, and cleaning it up would be a job. I could get paid for that. And with so many parking lots in Tampa I could get me a lot of work. As long as I don't let anybody else steal my idea.

So I'm extra amped when I pull up in front of Art's place on my Huffy after school. It's a beat-up bike the color of Cheetos with a useless back brake. To make a sudden stop without flying over the handlebars, you gotta stay crouched low while squeezing the left brake.

Jason and Ruben are fighting on the porch. I don't even notice who starts it half the time but it always ends with white jokes and short jokes. The bikes leaning against the building couldn't be more different—Ruben's rust on wheels and Jason's is brand-new, black with gray details, front and back pegs, so dope I still can't get over it.

Jason bought it himself, which is the coolest thing ever. His mom waits tables at some sports bar on the Hillsborough River—dartboards and baskets of food, a dozen TVs going. On weekends Jason helps out by shucking oysters and changing kegs.

Jason don't need basketball like we do. Give that loner a BMX bike and he'll freestyle all day, sometimes far from Maesta, in a park or the parking lot of the closed-down Winn-Dixie. I've always wondered how he can do that for hours, nobody but him around.

Now that he's replaced his stolen bike, we'll probably see him less.

"She moved away!" Ruben's saying. "That's why I didn't get with her."

Jason laughs and shakes his head. Turning to me he says, "Hey, it's Future Success boy."

"Hey, Whiteboy," I say.

I decided to tell them about the course instead of inventing detention every Friday. They didn't make too many jokes and Obie told me it was dope. Even congratulated me like I'd gotten first draft-pick into the Heat.

And *I* think his dealing drugs is stupid and don't say nothing. After more than a week delivering, he says it's a cinch, but all you need is that one guy who wants to rip you off, or that junkie who needs his fix. My boy could end up dead and instead of telling him to stop I'm all, "Dope kicks."

Jason's shaking his head at something Ruben said.

Ruben aims all his hate at Jason. "You jealous."

"Of your virtual girlfriend?"

And so on, Whiteboy having a blast and Ruben getting madder.

They talking about the latest internet girl he met through Instagram. Ruben's forever getting on the library computer to check out pics and hit up cute girls at other schools, and sometimes they hit him back.

He's a good-looking guy. That's just fact. Girls look at him, look away, then look again. On his page they can scope him out more, see him shirtless in some selfies, see his thick chest and rock abs. But in person girls notice he's short.

Jason gives a lazy "Whatever, little man," and spits on the dirt.

Ruben's bushy eyebrows bunch up.

How come it's okay to forever trash someone and then, one day, the same words spark rage? That's happened to all of us. Once Ruben kicked me for making fun of his mom's accent. When Art got the fake Nikes with the upside-down swoosh, Jason kept calling them "Sikes" and got put into a fierce headlock until he took it back.

Ruben turns to me. "Cool sneakers, bitch," he says, changing the subject.

I show him my favorite finger.

Jason's also looking at my left sneaker, at the quarter-sized hole over my big toe. A square of duct tape covers it from the inside, sticky side up, the light gray of the tape's back just about matching the dirty white Adidas.

"Bring them to my mom," Ruben says. "She can sew a cute smiley face patch over the hole."

I left the tape in but what can I do about my worn-down soles? I hop over puddles when it rains, but my socks get soaked anyway.

Art's coming around the building, pushing his seatless bike. He's got on his only decent shirt, a black button-up he wore to his brother Cedric's funeral.

Nothing bums me out more than thinking about Cedric, dead at seventeen. The bullet that was meant for someone else. On the news they said Cedric was in the wrong place at the wrong time, but he was two blocks from school a few minutes after being let out. Exactly where he was supposed to be. At the exact time.

They never caught the shooter. Nobody wanted to snitch.

Before the sadness creeps up on me I gotta bust a joke. I come up with "This ain't the prom, bitch."

"Yeah," Ruben says. "You looking for a job or going to court?"

"Gonna charm the managers, bitches. Make an impression so they remember me."

"They'll remember ya as the ghetto kid with the shirt fancy." Ruben cocks his head to the side while figuring out his mistake. "I mean *fancy shirt*."

"Who is ghetto?" Art asks in a perfectly white voice. "I will speak properly to the managers."

That cracks us up.

We hop on our bikes, cut behind building H, and right away spot something on the side of building M. It's a graffiti mural with tons of colors and swirls that might mean something. Why does it feel like I should get it?

Metallic blue on the edges. Curves of red in there. Splashes of orangey yellow. It's what my art teacher last year would call *abstract*, a word that means you ain't figuring it out.

Instead of a squiggly line, the tag's as beautiful as the rest of the art—a metal hook piercing a ball of fire. Keep staring and you see the flames flicker and fade and burst, you know, how fire changes nonstop but is always fire.

Crazy how something out there can match what I'm feeling inside. This piece gets me.

"Shit's amazing," Ruben says.

Art wonders if this genius was on LSD or something stronger. Jason says the guy has big balls, bombing in our hood.

True. Some guys around here will kick your ass for not belonging. I can't imagine the beatdown you'd catch for coming here to bomb a building that ain't yours.

Ruben says the guy's taunting us. "'Cause ya know it took hours."

They laugh when I tell them it could be a girl.

In the riot of colors I see eyes, right there in the middle, really sad or maybe tired. I got no idea what they, what any of it means.

I love the smooth glide of my bike, the wind whistling in my ears and blowing through my T-shirt, the distance I can cover without wearing down my kicks.

Obie ain't allowed out past six on a school night so just four of us are rolling one behind the other in the warm, sticky air. Cars zip past, the asphalt rushes beneath us, and our bikes cast long shadows on the sidewalk and parking lots, turning us into monsters on stretchy wheels.

We don't go riding much anymore since we stopped being little kids, but when exactly was that? There should be an official end-of-childhood day, one last time to play with Legos, pretend to be superheroes, and make up complicated handshakes. Then the next day you can start worrying about money, your virginity status, and if your breath stinks.

Every palm tree we pass makes me think of the book I'm supposed to read for English. It has a tree on the cover. That's all I know 'cause I ain't even cracked it open.

Oh, well. Making money's more important.

They say money changes people. No kidding. I could have more shirts, keep my hair decent. Plus extra money to go out. Not that I'm gonna ask Amy on a fancy-pants date or nothing, but while hanging out she could get thirsty or hungry, and whether at the 7-Eleven or McDonald's I gotta stand tall like a gentleman, dig into my pocket and be all, "Let me get that."

"You best not fuck this up for me," Art tells us for the third time. He needs us to be chill in the parking lots while he goes inside to chat up the managers.

Again we promise, put it on our moms' lives, which I never have a problem doing.

At the first shopping center, Art hits the Hungry Howie's while I go into the CVS. I'm thinking if someone's going to pay for me to sweep, it will be the biggest business here.

"Excuse me, is the manager around?" I ask.

The lady looks up from the cash she's bundling into a zipper bag and says, "That's me."

When I offer to sweep the parking lot she tells me that she could get an employee to do it. "Or else I'd have to pay you out of my own pocket."

I wait.

"Which I wouldn't do."

Right. Why would she? I need to try smaller businesses, where the owner is around.

After Art comes out we keep riding up Dale Mabry, along more traffic, getting a little sweaty. Nobody has taken off their shirts yet, which I never like to do. I'm all skin and bones, no curves on my arms or nowhere else. If not for my nipples, you wouldn't know where my stomach ends and my chest begins.

This could be a new city now with how different the buildings are. Bright-colored shopping plazas, no-litter parking lots, restaurants without drive-thrus, banks instead of check-cashing places.

At our tenth stop Art goes into Taco Bell and I dash over to the Chinese buffet, the smell of all that deliciousness hitting me at once. "All You Can Eat" is what the sign outside says, and I'd take that challenge, fill up my plate just like that guy in the Bucs jersey who's balancing an egg roll on his food mountain.

I've always wanted to sit down in a restaurant to order food from a menu in my hands, but this is way better. Take what you want and no waiting.

I could work here. There's a lot to do. Sweep the bits

of food on the floor. Wipe the tables. Take those dishes in back to wash. Everything I do at home I can do here.

I walk over to the Chinese lady at the cash register. Standing straight and with my professional voice full of respect, I tell her I can clear the tables, sweep and mop the floors, wash the dishes.

"I have enough employees."

"I'll do it for cheaper."

She laughs at that. When I don't laugh, to make it clear I'm serious, she gives me a fake smile.

So I offer to sweep the parking lot. Lucky for me you can see some litter from here, edged against the curb separating this plaza from the other.

She waves her husband over. He looks suspiciously at me as he listens to her Chinese. She's using a lot of words to say "This kid wants to sweep the parking lot."

Finally he says, "You clean parking lot?"

"Yes."

"Saturday morning, when no cars here, you sweep. Okay?"

"Okay." He's gone before I can thank him. The man didn't even tell me his name or how much he'd give me.

I rejoin my boys outside the Taco Bell, happy about my job but a little bummed that I gotta wait for the weekend. Amy won't see me with a fresh new look.

Ruben, standing in the shade of the drive-thru menu, says, "The heat has welded my nuts to my left leg."

I pull at the front of my shirt, where it clings to a wet spot in the middle of my chest. "Don't need status updates on your nuts."

I'm thirsty again. During the third stop at the supermarket, we all gathered our jingle of coins for the purified water machine. We stuck our heads in there one at a time, mouths aimed upward. On my turn most of it splashed on my face and shirt. It felt great.

Jason busts another turn on his bike and goes for a front pogo, his rear wheel popping up. He slows to a stop. "Art's either getting a job right now or fapping in the bathroom."

"I'm rooting for the first one," I say.

Nothing from Ruben. Since beefing with Jason earlier he ain't talked much. I wanna ask him if he's alright, but we don't ask each other stuff like that.

Sometimes you dis someone hard and people are all, "I can't believe you went there." So many topics are like that—places we ain't allowed to visit.

Me, I'm still thinking about Amy pretty much nonstop. If this gets any worse, I won't be able to walk, talk, or function in any normal way. Basketball don't take my mind off her, and this trip out here ain't doing it neither.

Jason stops wheeling around to watch two girls coming over here, crossing the lot from the supermarket. Too bad for Ruben that it's Gisela and her cousin.

Gisela takes off her sunglasses—blue eye shadow over brown eyes—and smiles. "Hey guys, what ya doing here?"

"Looking for hot girls." I scan the parking lot. "Can't find none so we better go."

They laughing so I guess the cousin has learned some English. While they both Colombian, only the cousin's *from* Colombia, still takes them immigrant classes.

Weird that I'm cool around girls I know, or when I ain't trying to hook up, or when I know I can't anyway. But put me in front of a girl I'm into and I become a stuttering, shaky fool.

"Wassup with you two?" Jason says.

"Her mom's shopping for the lady she works for," Gisela says. "We're getting something to eat."

Ruben's ignoring both of them though he could have a shot with the short cousin. His Spanish is perfect, unlike mine. I'd need a bilingual dictionary or an interpreter to talk to the newly arrived girls.

"Catch ya guys around," Gisela says, and we watch their bare legs until they disappear behind the tinted glass door of the Taco Bell.

Jason grins. "My future wife's hot."

Can't blame him for saying that around Ruben. He don't know what went down.

Halfway into last semester, me and Ruben was sitting in the back of geography when this new girl in tight-ass jeans walked in and sat down next to him, on the only free seat. One question from the hottie—*Where's the teacher?*—and they was vibing.

What other kid can chat up girls that easy? Most of us

need an introduction, and then we take super-slow, super-tiny baby steps to throwing game. Or else we tell a friend to tell her friend something and keep our fingers crossed.

After class, Gisela wrote her name and number on Ruben's folder, dotted the *i* with a tiny heart. But when he called that evening she couldn't talk, and the next day she somehow found another seat, closer to the front.

Though he shrugged it off, called her a tease, we both knew the deal.

Girls will go out with a boring guy, a pimpled guy, even a complete asshole. But if you're their height or shorter, you might as well give up.

Whiteboy lands a 180 bunny hop and brakes. "Her cousin's also fine," he says, putting one foot on the ground. "Too bad I don't *habla español*. Ruben, why didn't you ask them girls to check out your Instagram?"

Ruben's squinting at him.

"And let them see you shirtless, check out all your miniature bodybuilding muscles." Jason laughs. "Ya can hook up just like with them other girls."

"Shut up."

"Ruben the pimp-midget Cuban."

Ruben's off his bike and charging. He throws a right hook. Jason bends outta the way, he and his bike crashing on the asphalt.

These idiots! We promised Art!

Before Jason gets up I rush to bear-hug Ruben who

easily shoves me off. I tell them both to chill—a total waste of breath. This is already a fight, my two boys squared up and circling.

Though Jason can throw hands and is tall with crazy long reach, Ruben lifts every day, can probably hit harder. A pretty even match. What else can I do but watch and come up with Joe Rogan–type predictions?

Ruben throws a jab and misses. When a fist catches him on the forehead he staggers back. Now he's raging forward, thick arms pumping, and shoulder-slams Jason against a Ford Explorer, whose long legs are air-bound for a second. The alarm goes off.

The dozen people in Taco Bell are on their feet watching Jason and Ruben get tangled on the asphalt. Gisela and her cousin have come out for a better view. My boys are flopping around, one arm holding on tight while the other tries to land a punch, both refusing to let go. It's getting pathetic.

The stocky black manager with a tie and name tag rushes outta the Taco Bell shouting, "This is a family restaurant!"

Art trails behind, looking angrier.

The man pulls Jason and Ruben apart with ease. "Both of you just take it easy, alright?"

But this fight ain't over. Not even close. We gotta get the hell outta here, but these idiots are circling the man, murderous eyes locked, waiting for a clean shot.

Art's watching this with a bagged black shirt in his hand. He got the job! Wait, will he lose it now? I notice the huge stitch job on the side of his jeans, the jeans that'll soon rip somewhere else, eventually be unfixable, and though I ain't supposed to get sad for myself, much less for others, I can't help it. I feel something inside me break into a hundred pieces.

"Peace it out," I tell the dumbfucks. Then *I* do something super stupid. I turn to Art again, for a moment too long, and with that the manager knows we all here together.

"We already called the cops," the man says, standing between the fighters again.

All four fists drop.

The manager goes and snatches the black shirt from Art's hand. "You get lost too."

Art's staring down at his empty hands like he's lost in a dream or like there really is something in them, maybe a crystal ball showing him the future.

The rest of us shout for him to hurry, already on our bikes.

"Cops" is all we had to hear.

9

LATER THAT week, outside of Future Success, I slap hands
with Zach and bump fists, without thinking, like he's my
homie from Maesta or something.

He says, "Ready to succeed?"

"Yep."

He has one of them old-school *abuelo* shirts today.

"Nice guayabera," I tell him.

"*Muchas gracias*," he says, smoothing down the rows of
pleats on his black shirt.

I noticed him during lunch today, rehearsing some
sorta play with two girls on the grass between halls. I mention that to him.

"Yeah, it's for a play coming up. You should come."

I'm thinking about the few times I've had to get in front
of a classroom to speak, and that's no more than thirty
kids. "Ain't you nervous in front of all them people?"

"I probably will be, but I have to get used to it. I want to be a professional actor."

He's the second kid I know who has his future planned. Obie is sure he'll be a physicist. How about *me*? I can't think of a single thing I'd like to do besides basketball, and I probably won't be good enough for the NBA.

Zach tells me that he's got a big box of clothes and hats at home, stuff from the Salvation Army. Just for fun, all by himself, he'll sometimes act out favorite movie scenes.

I gotta give him props, confessing to that weirdness.

"Move it!" says a girl's voice.

I check behind me. It's my girl Amy, blowing a bubble with her gum. Just before the expanding pink bubble touches her nose she pops it.

I step away from the doorway to let her pass. If she's being an asshole to me, maybe I should be an asshole to her. Would that work?

The bell rings and we head inside.

I had the two-seater table to myself last week but now Zach sits next to me. So we hanging out during this class. Afterward, it's gonna be harder to talk to Amy but it's on no matter what. It's just me and my ratty gray tee, my holey sneakers, and whatever comes to mind.

Today Breckner ain't pacing. Straight as a flagpole, he says, "Let's consider some statistics. Out of the two hundred and thirty-three sophomores in this school, at least two of you will be lawyers or teachers. At least one of you will be an engineer. Another will be a surgeon. These are the good jobs that require education. Many of you will work terrible jobs for terrible wages. The choice is yours."

Yep, he's talking about the future again.

I guess he don't think our lives are real yet, that what I'm dealing with is only preparation for what's coming.

He holds up them scary green sheets of paper. "I have asked your teachers for progress reports based on the first weeks of the semester." He walks up and down the rows handing out the unofficial report cards, also thick envelopes for our parents.

It's all Fs on my sheet except for one C, thanks to Mr. Dawson. He's the fresh-out-of-college teacher who promised me easy grades in geography if I could hook him up just once, so he could find a local connection. When he called my name after class that day I thought I was in trouble, but he was just a new guy in town wanting to score weed.

On the bottom of the sheet, the teacher comments say, *Doesn't put in enough effort* and *Doesn't do homework.*

The usual. It makes me sound lazy in general which I'm not. I spend hours looking for work and would spend hours working if somebody would pay me. It's just that school don't make much sense no matter how much I try to pay attention or care about homework.

"These envelopes contain information about Future Success. It's for your parents to look over, in case they haven't or can't visit the website."

That's my mom—hasn't and can't. And won't.

"You need to buckle down and get your grades up immediately. Okay, people? Though you all have great potential, you won't achieve success until you tap into it. You need to care about yourselves as much as your teachers and parents care."

A few huffs rise. Some kids are shaking their heads all pissed off. Amy lets out a "Yeah, right!" and I cough out the word "Bullshit!" at the same time, but she don't notice. She's hunched over her notebook, doodling. Openly ignoring Breckner.

Our reactions stun him. I'm sorta surprised too. With so many kids here on the principal's shit list, I figured this class would slip into chaos quick, but so far it's been chill, no reason to press the red button.

Breckner's gaze sweeps over the room like he lost something. "Excuse me?"

Not one word from us.

Amy raises her head from the notebook and brushes the bangs away from her eyes. "Mr. Breckner? No offense or nothing, but you're talking out your butt." She's staring him down like with Uppercut on that day I fell in love.

"Yeah." This from the normally mute goth kid by the pencil sharpener. "You don't know squat about our parents and teachers."

The room goes rowdy with everybody agreeing.

"Okay, people. Settle down."

We start to and Breckner gets back on his positive kick. That smiling's gotta be like a stutter—hard to get rid of.

"All I'm asking is for you to consider your futures. It may be fun to live carefree but the future is coming. It's coming whether you're ready or not."

Just like last Friday it's future, future, future. I can't stand it anymore. I wish a time machine could zap Breckner into the future and keep him there.

He tells us we'll do an activity and gets to handing out the sheets of paper. "Where do you see yourselves in five, ten years?" The handout in front of me says "Life Map" on the top. Blank spaces all over, diagonal arrows connecting them.

"How do you plan to achieve your goals?" he asks, setting a handout beside Amy's notebook. "What is it you want?" He hands one to a kid who mumbles something.

Me, I want Brian dead. Stabbed about a thousand times. Where's the blank space for that?

There's a space for college (four years) and a space for a master's degree (another two years). I try to picture me in one of them super-smart colleges where ropy plants crawl over the old brick buildings. At the graduation ceremony my mom shows up 'cause you can't shrug off success like that, can't help but take proud photos of your son in a judge robe and square hat.

How come it's so hard to hold them thoughts in my head? It could happen, I guess, though most people in

Maesta go to jail instead of college. I don't know nobody who's gone past high school. Don't even know anybody with a really good job besides Carlos, Jason's neighbor, who manages the Dollar Mart. He walks around the air-conditioned store rocking a vest and tie, with a card attached to a string on a belt loop for swiping through cash registers. Carlos gives orders to the workers or else hangs out in the office, but how good's that job, really, if he's still living in Maesta?

Breckner says, "First jot down a few professions that appeal to you. It could be anything as long as—" He narrows his eyes at Amy, who ain't even glanced at the handout yet. So focused on her drawing that she don't notice Breckner going over to her.

"Doodle another time!" Breckner closes her notebook.

The room goes quiet. Amy, mouthy with kids and grown-ups, just sits there looking up at him, open jawed, nothing in her mouth but air.

Last week Breckner had our attention and now that it's gone, so is his smile. He's pissed. Watching him do that to Amy, I'm also pissed. I wanna stand up for her. For me too. I wanna be brave like she was with Uppercut.

"All we ever do is talk about the stupid future," I say. "How 'bout the present?"

A bunch of comments pop up, stuff like "Yeah!" and "That's right!"

Amy turns, like she feels what I'm saying.

I hope she does. The world's so fucked that my imagination can't reach past the three years before my life becomes my own. Zach's gotta be feeling hopeless too. Teachers want him to solve equations, memorize dates, and write stupid information in stupid blank spaces, all while his mom might die in the next second.

Every eye in the room's on me. All you hear is Breckner's shoes squeaking over. He ain't tall, especially for a grown man, but right now, standing in front of me, he's eight feet of towering teacher rage. "I need everybody's attention, Marcos. We are not to be doodling. We are considering our futures."

I stare back at Breckner, the idiot. What should I tell him? I could say that picturing the future's hard when messing with today takes all you got. That doodling feels good. It might be the best thing we can do, letting something inside us come out.

But saying that to a teacher? With everybody staring?

So I show him my middle finger. "Consider *this*!"

The classroom explodes with cheers and applause. Mess with the girl I like, that's how I do it.

Then my heart starts beating like mad. What's gonna happen to me?

Breckner comes over to me so quick I think he's gonna punch me or something. He makes the get-up gesture, palm up, fingers closing over it twice. He just wants me out.

As he's leading me out the door to the sound of all that

applause, I feel like a hero. For Amy and everybody else.

I sit on the hall floor by the drinking fountain to wait for class to end. Me and Zach walk home together—that's my excuse, but mostly I'm thinking about Amy and how much easier it will be talking to her now.

From here I see the fish tank through the glass wall of the principal's office. I get up and walk over there. The office is empty, looks almost peaceful. As usual, the fish don't seem to notice me. Nobody expects anything from these guys, swimming around a tank. Must be nice.

I count fourteen again, and wonder if Breckner will kick me out of his class for good and if I'd even care if it wasn't for Amy. I think I would. I don't love talking about the future or staying an extra half hour every Friday, but I like that someone believed in me enough to put me in that class.

I wanna believe in me too.

The class door opens. Here they come, all smiles, telling me how great that was, giving me the thumbs-up. Two kids high-five me. The metalhead who hangs with Amy nods as he passes.

Amy trails behind them and sticks around. After everybody except Zach takes off she walks up.

"That was awesome."

She really just said that. Used that word. And since I did that awesome thing maybe that makes me awesome?

"Thanks."

"For real, I'd totally slap your palm but I don't do high fives."

Zach grins like a villain. "You can kiss him."

Amy laughs. Her in front of me and that sweet sounding laugh is better than a million congratulations from a million kids.

"What's your name?" she says.

"Marcos Rivas." I actually say both names and hold my hand out.

A dorky move. Now what? Dropping my hand would be doing the robot so might as well leave it there, between us.

"Wow. Formal." She pumps my hand up and down twice, like I just sold her a car. "Amy Carrington. Pleasure to meet you."

I roll with her joke and say, "This is my associate, Zach."

"Hi." Then he turns to me. "Gotta get something from my locker." He takes off, and I almost love him for that.

It's only me and Amy in the hall now.

"I know you just spoke your mind in there," Amy says. "But you also spoke my mind. Plus you flipped him off, so thank you."

"No problem."

"I didn't say anything because . . . I don't know. I was in shock." She moves her binder from one hand to the other. "He's usually super nice. Clueless, but at least he seems to give a shit."

Is that true? He's got enthusiasm, that's for sure, always

trying to give us some, pushing us to do better in all them classes that ain't got nothing to do with him.

"I guess that's true," I say. "He cares, but not for doodling."

We start toward the school exit, passing the computer club kids in room 208.

"It's only us and the after-school nerds here," I say.

"We're sorta after-school nerds too." I love the way she says *we*.

"Sorta," I say. "Breckner and some teachers think we got nerd potential."

We walking and talking so naturally it's almost like I could reach over and hold her hand.

Zach's waiting by the "Welcome to Hanna High" bulletin board. "Have you two kissed yet?"

"Turn around," Amy tells him, twirling a finger in the air.

I laugh while Zach actually turns around and Amy rolls her eyes. I'm still laughing when Amy plants a kiss on my cheek.

It's a speedy peck but it's the greatest thing that's ever happened to me.

10

ME AND Amy sitting together at our own cafeteria table, her giving me the rest of her fries, us hanging out at the mall, at her house, us mixing with each other's friends— ain't none of that happened yet.

I know a kiss don't magically turn a girl into your girl- friend, especially if it's a peck on the cheek, not a make-out session. Still, I expected something. To at least talk and get to know her. But I've barely seen her around school in the six days since that kiss.

I ain't been able to think of anything else. On Saturday I swept the parking lot of the Chinese buffet. Mr. Zeng paid me ten bucks and told me try back in a month. With the money I already had, that was enough for a haircut and a new solid black T-shirt, which I'm wearing now.

Looking as sharp as I've ever looked, I'm feeling pretty good, and I ain't trying to wait for Future Success tomorrow.

When the last bell rings I bolt over to 127, the art room, where I saw Amy go in a few weeks back.

When I spot the back of her head coming outta there, the brown hair with blue streaks, I take longer, quicker steps to catch up. Then I slow down to run into her by chance.

"Hey, Amy."

She stops. "Marcos Rivas."

We stand in the middle of the hall as kids stream past us on either side. Her smile jumbles up my brain. I can't think of what to say, can't remember *what* I planned to say. If I had a plan at all.

"So . . . Amy . . . wanna hang out sometime?"

She's considering it, giving me an extra-slow nod that might last forever. What's coming will either make me crazy happy or make me wanna take a running dive off the school roof.

"Okay," she says. "Follow me."

She means *now*. Being real with this girl works! We walking through noise and bodies. What if my boys see us? I don't wanna explain Amy until there's a reason to.

"Where we going?" I ask her.

"Someplace private."

I see Art toss a book into his locker while Obie waits with a fully loaded backpack. He'll drop the books off at his aunt's, stuff the backpack up with drugs, do the deliveries, then grab his books again before going home.

With his job and the Bible study and church twice a

week and the homework he does, I hardly see him any-more. Good money or not, it makes no sense for one of the best students in school to be dealing.

Art spots me first and then Obie looks over. Later, if my boys ask, I'll tell them we was going to detention.

Super popular Tina and her two hot friends, the Tina Trio, are coming our way. They teen-movie popular, the sophomore version, and move through the halls like they doing you a big favor by being there. As always, I try not to look. Let the other guys fall over each other to stare with tongues and eyes popping out. I ain't with giving these stuck-ups the satisfaction.

"Those girls are the worst," Amy says, and zags left.

The trio come to a sudden stop.

Amy beams a huge smile at them. "Hi, skanks."

A thrill shoots through me. *Now* I'm watching closely.

Tina's eyes sweep down Amy's body and back up. "Excuse me?"

"Your outfits are adorable," Amy says in an extra-girly voice. "I'll come over later than usual today to listen to crappy pop music and invent rumors to spread. I'm gonna get a spray tan first so I can be bright orange like you."

After a moment of shocked silence Tina says, "What-ever."

"What's the deal with *you*?" Amy asks the other two. "I called you *all* skanks. Does Queen Skank need to give you permission to speak?"

Say that to a Maesta girl and she'll take off her earrings, but here the Tina Trio just stand around blinking.

The one with the braces finally says, "Who are you?"

"I'm the girl you were talking about during lunch today. My friend heard it." She's looking all hard at each girl. "So now I'm giving you a chance to say it to my face." When their cheeks go red Amy says, "Thought so."

And we take off. I'm laughing and following Amy as she turns down the other hall.

"That was great," I tell her. "You're my hero."

"Now we're even."

When we outside and passing the gym it hits me that she might be . . . No way. Really? Could she be taking me to the dugout? Why are my palms sweating?

Stuff happens in the dugout. Secret stuff like your best friend showing you molly, meth, and weed in his backpack. Plus less secret things like people making out during school dances or Alex and Liz banging, according to rumors. Now I wonder if it's a place where love can show up.

We cross the baseball field. Step inside the dugout and sit on the cracked plank of wood.

She says, "I'm not a big fan of the sun."

I *love* the sun, could be president of its fan club, but I don't say nothing.

She unzips a coin purse and pulls out a tiny pipe, grainy and gray like a stone.

"I pinch so little that my mom never notices."

"Cool."

And I guess it *is* cool though I ain't into weed. It can make you forget your sadness, sure, and gets you thinking big important thoughts. But when the high becomes low your mood drops and it hits you that the thoughts wasn't very big or important.

A breeze comes through carrying Amy's sweet scent. I wonder if it's her soap, shampoo, perfume, or a bunch of scents that make her smell like a basket of fruit.

She hands over the packed pipe with the lighter. I take a big toke, the smoke warm and thick in my lungs until they feel a pinch and I'm coughing.

"Lightweight," she says. "Don't you guys 'spark blunts' all the time?" She giggles at that.

"Funny," I say. "Don't ya punks usually shoot heroin with shared needles?"

Which gets me a smile.

Right away the weed's lifting me, shedding my nervousness. But that's just how it starts. Weed makes other things better. If aspirin's for headaches and backaches, then weed might be for all the hurt that comes from having nobody to vibe with, from empty fridges and mean words shot your way on the daily, from pushing the pain deep down when it's trying to tear itself out.

When you high, that stuff don't matter. When you high, that stuff don't even exist.

As my brain buzzes beautifully, I look past the baseball

field to the blue sky in the distance, above the squat houses across the street, the sunshine bright on everything except us, me and Amy, in the cool shade of the dugout. Everywhere the talk of birds fills the warm air.

The grass sparkles with water spurting from the jerky sprinklers going *tak, tak, tak,* such an amazing sound, the sunlight catching in the water, flashing rainbows, such an amazing sight, and what an amazing thing water is, so necessary 'cause we drink it, 'cause it drops from clouds so plants and food can grow, and it hits me that water's the only thing in the world that can't get wet, 'cause that's what water *is.*

"Dude, you're way high."

I snap into the world again to notice Amy staring at me. "Not really."

"Shoulda seen your face. Like you were figuring out the secret of the universe. Or taking a dump."

"I was thinking."

I feel like telling her my thoughts. Why does weed do that to me? Smoking with Obie that one time I got to talking about God. I told my boy that I wanted to believe but it was hard, that praying didn't work or maybe I wasn't doing it right. I even described my technique. Obie said he was no expert but how you kneel or sit or what you do with your hands don't matter. You just gotta believe, he said.

And maybe that don't sound like a big deal, us discussing

God, but we'd never done that before. It's like weed made that conversation happen.

And now I'm wondering, What if weed don't make you high at all? Maybe it makes the surface bullshit fall away and you become the kid underneath, the one you're meant to be, and that *feeling* of freedom is what lifts you.

Or maybe I'm higher than an astronaut.

"So are you kicked out of the class now?" Amy extends the pipe, still lit, a circle of fire orange under gray ash. I notice the chipped green polish on her nails.

I turn down that third toke. "I hope I ain't kicked out." Right away I hear it. I shoulda said "I don't know" and left it at that. Now it sounds as if I like the class, want to be there. Liking and wanting some things ain't cool.

Amy says, "I'm still wondering which teacher chose me for it."

"Same here."

She hits the pipe again, holds it in, and then blows smoke into the glittering sunshine. "What do boys think about anyway, besides sex and video games?"

"Don't know. I'm just me, I guess. I ain't in a club or nothing."

"Yeah. I guess I don't have much in common with other girls."

She puts the pipe and lighter into the coin purse, which she then stuffs in the side pocket of her raggedy green cargo shorts. A rip on the bottom's sewn up with a darker green thread. Not a bad job though I can do it better. I've noticed Amy's clothes these last weeks and she don't got many more than me. Amy's poor.

I'm thinking about that whole judging-book-covers thing and how me and Amy could have more in common than me and a Maesta girl. Maybe I really do got a shot.

Focus, Marcos. What seemed impossible before, Amy next to you, is happening right now and you ain't all the way here.

I say, "Maybe there ain't no such thing as the typical boy or the typical girl 'cause we all different on the inside but trying to be the same on the outside so we don't feel alone."

Amy's looking at me. In my head I go over the words I've said. Was it crazy space-cadet stuff? "Or maybe I think about things too much."

"No."

"People tell me that all the time."

"People are stupid," she says. "What you said was smart."

I'm high on Amy's weed and her closeness, and now her words lift me even higher. Me and her in this quiet shade, less than an arm's reach away . . . it'd be the most romantic thing in the world if kids wasn't passing by.

"Ow!" an emo kid shouts, and holds the back of his head, where he just got slapped by his friend.

The three sophomores passing by, hauling backpacks,

jeans tight on their skinny legs, see us and look surprised. They don't know me but might know Amy. I wonder if we gotta worry about tomorrow. If *Amy's* gotta worry, I mean. While rumors of us alone in the dugout could destroy her rep, it could only skyrocket mine.

She starts talking about their emo music, how some of it ain't bad. Tells me original punk, her favorite, is the best, that the new stuff's cute and from the suburbs.

"With me it's hip-hop and the Smiths," I say, "but I'd like to listen to your music sometime."

"I love the Smiths! You know, Morrissey started out doing punk."

"Nice," I say. "Didn't know that."

Amy tells me she listens to some rap, old stuff like N.W.A and Public Enemy. "I can get into anything, even some of the old country music my grandma plays."

Country? If we not into the same stuff, the least I could do is be open to it, like with the punk music. But country? I can't help laughing. "For real?"

"Why's that funny? I gotta be wearing a cowboy hat to like country music?"

"That's right! You gotta be wearing a cowboy hat *and* boots *while* taming a wild horse to like country music. Ain't no other way."

But she busted me. I *was* thinking of her dressed up like she lived on a Texas ranch. What if when I mentioned hip-hop she thought of drive-by shootings and booty clapping?

"Seriously," Amy says. "Some people think that only one thing defines us. Look how school cliques get organized that way. It's bullshit."

"You're right," I say. "It's dumb."

Worst of all, it's why the idea of me and Amy together sometimes don't make sense. Even though we make a bunch of sense.

So me and her are anti-cliques. We should start a campaign! Post a video on YouTube! Write the president a letter! No more categories for kids. No more sections in cafeterias. I wanna tell her my genius ideas—all around the world teenagers hanging with whoever they want.

Man, I'm blazed.

I say, "Categories are stupid."

"Yep. I thought so in junior high but in high school it's worse."

"A little more than two years left."

And I'm trying to finish those years like everybody else. I remember the row of Fs on that sheet of paper.

Amy lies on the bench, her Chucks two inches from me. All over them she's Sharpied designs, names of bands, even an *I* ♥ *M*. Does *M* stand for Misfits? It's a band shirt she wears a lot, the one with the skull logo.

She's staring at the planks of wood above us. "You know what's messed up?"

That we here together? Please don't think it's messed up. "What?"

She says, "In high school we're supposed to be one way, so we fit in, and at home we gotta be another way, for our parents. We can never be ourselves."

"Yeah, that's right," I tell her. Now I'm wondering, who'd I be if I could be myself? "I don't know who I am half the time," I say. "If nobody was looking, if I was the last person on earth, who would I be? Maybe my real life should be different. Maybe the opposite."

Amy takes that all in as I wonder if all those words were too many.

She giggles. "Bizarro Marcos."

It's like she's waiting for me to laugh too.

"I don't get it," I tell her.

"You know, like Bizarro Superman?"

"I don't read comics."

Amy explains Bizarro Superman, the evil twin, first in the comic book and how he later showed up in the cartoon. "The point is, he totally looks like Superman and has the same powers, but is opposite in every other way."

If I could choose, maybe I'd give up this handed-to-me life and become totally different. What if I'd been born knowing my dad? What if I'd been born in a place where basketball and hip-hop ain't popular? Who would I be?

How dope it'd be to escape the things that made me, but where could I go?

Amy folds a leg under her to face me better. "What would be the opposite of your life?"

A good question. I give it some thought. "A kid living in a mansion, whose fun-loving pop helps him practice golf putts in the backyard."

"Snooze."

I agree. Say what you want about my life but it ain't boring.

"I guess the opposite of me would be one of the Tinas," Amy says. "Whichever one tans the most."

"So we'd be hanging out in a Bizarro world. A Tina would kick it with a golf-playing Timothy."

We laugh at that.

"For you," Amy says, "what would be the opposite of right now?"

"This is a pretty great moment," I say, and try to think up something terrible. "Okay, check it out. The opposite of right now would be getting kicked in the nuts while listening to country music."

She's laughing hard so I bust up too. She's trying to hold it in for some reason, eyes closed, shoulders moving up and down—a cartoon laugh. It ain't the joke so much as the weed, which makes it funnier. When we finally catch our breath, the dugout's silent again.

I don't say nothing and it's like I ain't gotta, the silence enough for now, somehow pulling me closer to her than I already am. So close that if neither of us moved, maybe I could feel what she's feeling.

11

THE NEXT day, I walk into Future Success like last week never happened. What middle finger? The plan was to come in all natural and instead here I am *strolling* in, Sunday-in-the-park style, setting my weekly study report on Breckner's desk as I pass.

I've never strolled in my life. Never even used that word.

I go sit next to Zach. The other Future Success kids smile at me before turning to the teacher, who's still writing. Is Breckner gonna kick me out when he sees me?

Zach wonders the same thing, chin pointing at our teacher who still ain't looked up from his writing.

I answer with a shrug.

"The play's tomorrow night."

"I'm there," I say, and think about inviting Amy.

Like a mind reader he says, "Invite whoever you want."

"Yeah, I might invite Amy."

When Amy walks through the door I wave her over. She sets her study report on Breckner's desk before taking a seat on my other side, just across the aisle.

Check me out, hanging out with a theater boy and a punk girl.

"What's he doing with those study reports anyway?" Amy asks.

I've wondered the same thing. When Zach mentions he might verify them with our teachers, a worry sets in. Everything I write in them—the notes I take, the homework I do, the reading—is a lie. I'm just trying to do what I gotta in this class, so I can be with Amy.

I know the future's coming, like Breckner says. It's how I imagine it too, me staying put and the future heading my way like a beat-up van, full of who knows what. And sure it's a smart idea to be prepared for when that van stops and the door slides open, but I just can't get into school.

The starting bell rings and my heart pumps faster.

Worried for nothing, it turns out, 'cause he gets up, sees me, and starts class by explaining the three learning styles—visual, auditory, and tactile. We spend about fifteen minutes on a style indicator exam that classifies me as a visual learner. The advice is to review and rewrite class notes, make outlines and diagrams, all so my brain can hold on to things for tests.

"If we want to achieve success," Breckner tells us, "this

is the most important tool. Keep in mind how you learn best in order to study more effectively."

But *how* I study ain't my problem, and I bet it's the same for the others. We don't take class notes, don't do homework, don't care. Poor study habits? We don't study at all. Breckner and whoever sent him don't get that.

Future Success, my nuts. What a waste of time.

At the end of class Breckner says, "We have been invited by the Tampa Bay Rays to watch a home game when baseball season begins!"

At least half the class gets excited. Kids look around for other baseball fans or just people who want to see a baseball stadium. I get amped 'cause it's more time with Amy.

"Future Success kids from all over the district will be there," Breckner says.

That corny name for this class is bad enough and now he wants to call *us* that?

"There will be a bus ride from the school to Tropicana Field where we'll listen to a talk, have a meal, and watch the game."

A kid in the front row asks, "For free?"

"For free. It's six weeks away, but your parents need the information today. So they can mark that date and make the necessary arrangements to be there. You *must* bring a parent."

The kid by the window mumbles something about his parents being in rehab, and our confused teacher pauses like it might be a joke.

"Or a guardian," Breckner finally adds.

Who am I supposed to take? My mom would laugh at the idea of going anywhere with me, and taking one of my friend's moms would be straight weird.

Why don't I know any grown men? Why's Maesta just moms and kids? Chris and them who are forever drinking beer beside the bumping blue Mazda might jump at the chance to watch a ball game for free. But we ain't tight.

There's César, the old man who wanders shirtless around Maesta all "Hey, boss" to everybody, a bummed cigarette behind an ear. Or else he's at the corner Hess station in a shirt, offering to pump your gas or wash your windows, sometimes holding the door for you. Anything for a buck. If he'll wear a shirt to scrounge, he might wear one for a free ball game.

"Okay, people," Breckner says. "Have a great weekend."

I get up with everybody else and roll my folder into my fist.

"Marcos," Breckner says. "I'd like a word with you, please."

Here we go. One whole week to come up with a punishment and now he's gonna give it to me. Will it be a few days of detention? A week? Will he kick me out for good? Maybe it's worse than that. Maybe he's gonna give me a speech.

I'll dodge it with an apology. As soon as the classroom

empties, I walk over to him on wiggly legs.

"Sorry for flipping you off."

He unzips his backpack. "I hope that's true, Marcos."

It's my typical interaction-with-adults routine, saying what they wanna hear, but to my surprise it's also real talk. I *am* sorry.

He says, "I'm here to give help and it's impossible to do that when students don't want it."

As he puts his folder into the backpack I spot an empty lunch container and a book, a number on the spine. The food came from home and the book from some library.

It's got me remembering a couple summers back. While testing a new shortcut, me and Obie saw our fifth-grade teacher lifting Publix bags outta the trunk. On the front porch two little boys was jumping up and down like they'd explode if the door didn't open soon. Seeing her there shocked us even though it's normal for a lady to live in a house, normal for her to have kids, normal to buy food from a supermarket.

The lesson I learned? Teachers are people. Sometimes, though, you can forget that.

Breckner could be a regular guy, someone named Thomas or William. I'm just about to ask him . . .

"If you don't care about this program, you shouldn't be here." There's no anger in his voice.

"I wanna be here. I care."

Only the first part of what I said is true.

"Do you *really*, Marcos? This semester you haven't turned in a single homework assignment for algebra or history. I only had time to speak with two of your teachers today."

Breckner don't got much time 'cause he only comes on Fridays, but the other teachers would have told him the same.

"Are you applying anything you're learning in my class?"

Breckner thumbs through the weekly study reports on his desk until he finds mine. He hands it to me. The list of assignments on the left is real, but the details on the right, how I did them, the study principles I applied, are total bullshit.

"Do better, Marcos," he tells me.

"Okay, Mr. Breckner."

That's easy to say. It's not necessarily a *yes*. It could mean that I heard him and understand what he said.

His face has softened and he offers me his hand. No joke, we shaking on it.

"In that case I accept your apology. Let's not mention the matter again."

Gripping his big hand makes me feel like . . . what? More than a kid. More like a real person, I guess. How dope it'd be to shake all my teachers' hands.

Amy and Zach, talking up a storm, stop when they see me coming down the hall.

"We shook hands," I tell them. "We're good now."

Amy's impressed. "You're not in trouble?"

"Nah."

"Sweet," Zach says. "I'm gonna flip him off next week."

Amy says, "Now you can go to the baseball game."

She tells us that her mom is a superfan. "It will probably be cheesy as hell, with a bunch of motivational speeches. Please say you'll be there."

"I'm there." It's a promise now. I gotta find a guardian.

"Cool. I couldn't survive the game without you."

If only I coulda recorded that. I'd edit out "the game" part and listen to her voice all day. Crazy how some words can lift you higher than weed.

You'd think the three of us was best friends, about to head out for a movie or wherever, but it ain't like that at all. Zach and Amy just met, might soon be friends, and me and Amy . . . I wanna be more than friends.

Come to think of it, I ain't never had a friend who's a girl.

Handing me a flash drive she says, "I put some punk songs here for you to check out. You already listen to anti-establishment music, so I think you'll like this."

"Cool. Thanks." I turn the flash over in my hands, this thing that's warm from her pocket, full of songs she chose especially for me.

She says, "I'm out."

Always having to run and me always wanting to see

her. Our few minutes together after Future Success ain't enough.

"Let's hang out tonight," I say, looking only at her.

"Okay."

She tells me to text her, gives me her number, but I still don't got credit on my phone.

I think fast. "My phone's dead and I can't find my charger."

On the inside of my wrist she writes *412* in blue ink, holding my hand in hers, her thin fingers so soft and warm I almost close my eyes to feel them better.

"That's the apartment building. I live on the same street as the school, three blocks away."

"What apartment number?"

"Just throw pebbles like we're in an eighties movie," she says. "You'll know which window."

As she opens her arms for a hug, I tell myself not to hang on too long.

I put my arms around her lower back, and she puts hers around my shoulders. It's like a warm one-second bath. We let go at the same time. Then she hugs Zach.

I watch her move down the hall, ponytail bouncing.

Zach asks, "You're really into her, huh?"

A personal question. Like we tighter than tight. Not even my boys know about Amy and I'm supposed to tell Zach? For the last two Fridays we've walked home, just me and him, about thirty minutes of hanging out and not talking about the typical stuff that don't matter, like I do with my boys. Zach even told me about his mom having cancer, so maybe I can tell him something personal too. Maybe he can be a different sorta friend from my boys. Maybe my secret ain't gotta stay a secret.

"I'm really into her."

Didn't mean to blurt it out. Now I wait for some humiliation—a smile, a laugh, a joke. I'm also crazy curious. Gotta know how people will see me and Amy. By tomorrow night after the play, we could be boyfriend and girlfriend.

Zach's nodding like I just told him the time. "Cool."

And that's all he says. Weird. Or is it? If he ain't treating it like a big deal, maybe it ain't.

We start for home and he changes the subject. "So, are you a visual, auditory, or tactile learner?"

12

OUTTA ALL the bedroom distractions I've come up with since Brian moved in, ceiling ball's the best. How it works is you lie on the bed and toss a rolled-up sock into the air, trying to get within an inch of the ceiling for one point. Fall short or touch the ceiling and it's minus two. That's what I'm playing now, hitting fifty-seven points while "Search and Destroy" by the Stooges comes through my dinky speaker at a low volume.

> *And I'm the world's forgotten boy*
> *The one who's searchin', searchin' to destroy*

I like that the song ain't all, "Baby, I love being with you" or "Baby, why did you leave me?" which could be the titles for most songs.

Every minute I'm home I spend here, hiding from Brian, with no technology except for my stereo. What would I do without my MP3 speaker to keep me company?

I got one car to wash this weekend, an old man who asked me to come by once a month, and I might as well try everybody else in that neighborhood again. They mighta changed their minds. The parking lot idea hasn't worked a second time and Mr. Zeng from the Chinese restaurant also only needs me once a month.

I'll keep searching though.

A screaming song comes on. I'm still waiting for one love song, if they make punk love songs, or at least lyrics that mean something to me.

Today, my room don't feel as sad or lonely as usual. Here I can daydream without distractions. I'm imagining my date tonight with Amy, where we might go and what we might talk about, besides this punk music, which ain't too bad. It's actually pretty good.

Will tonight be me and Amy's second date? How do I know if walking to the dugout (five minutes) and the time in the dugout (thirty minutes) adds up to a date?

No clues come to me while listening to the lyrics until I'm up to sixty-two points at ceiling ball. It's a track that rocks softer than the others, the lyrics hard to understand except for the hook.

chunk of heart destroyed by quiet

yell it out before it kills you now
let it all out

The blue display reads Jawbreaker. Don't know whether that's a guy or the whole band, but those lyrics describe me. Those things I force myself to keep inside do feel like they destroying me. Is Amy telling me to let it out?

After the second hook, the lyrics go, "I want you, I want you, I—"

Brian barges in. "Turn that shit off!" His hand's still on the doorknob. "It's worse than the nigger noise you play."

The volume's low as always. I reach over and turn it off, my arm shaking.

Brian's staring at me. If I look back, I'm also staring, and he don't like that. If I don't look at him, I'm a disrespectful little bean nigger. That's why I'm sorta moving my eyes back and forth.

"Hand it over," he says, so calm it scares me.

"I'm sorry. I'll use it with headphones from now on."

"Give. It. To. Me."

Bad move. I really *am* a dipshit, making him say things twice. Three times and he'll snap. I get up from the bed and unplug the speaker. Does he want me to beg? I'll beg.

"I promise you'll never hear a sound from my room ever again," I tell him. "Please, pleeeease, Brian. I promise."

Between clenched teeth he says, "Give it to me right fucking now."

He steps closer and I hold out the speaker. "Here."

"Disrespect me again and I'll fuck you up. Got it?"

"Okay."

"Okay?"

"I swear. I won't disrespect you again."

And I mean it. I really do. I say the last part with all my soul so he understands.

He smiles. "Not as tough as you think, huh, dipshit?"

He takes the speaker with one hand, still breathing on me. With the other hand he makes a fist and brings it up fast. Punches me right in the nuts.

I drop to the floor. This pain's new, a grinding that reaches my stomach. He walks out. I'm twisting and turning on the carpet. That don't help so I lie curled up, which don't help neither. I wait for the grinding to end.

I get up after a few minutes, still hurting. Though I'm hungry, I won't go out to the kitchen unless my mom's home. She lets Brian get away with everything, but he still behaves better when she's here.

The only good thing about having Brian around is I ain't gotta take care of my mom no more. I always know where she is—at work or at home. Without a boyfriend, she used to go out at night and come home wasted, her Kia not always fitting neatly in the parking space.

Way past midnight, when the creaking front door would wake me, I'd listen for her steps in the hall. The time it took her to head over to her bedroom told me how hard I'd gotta shake her awake the next morning for work.

This one time, a week before my eleventh birthday, the front door opened and closed, no other sound. Sometimes she passed out on the couch so I got up to check. Found her lying in the middle of the living room floor, some guy with his back to me, hands lifting up her skirt.

I'm forever dreaming up action hero moments, me stepping up to the challenge and saving the day, but when I grabbed my bat I got too scared to use it. Instead, I shouted from the hallway in the deepest voice I could fake, "Get outta here before I fucking kill you!" He bolted out and drove away.

I put my mom's underwear back on her. Pulled down her skirt. After trying to lift her skinny body, I hated myself for being too weak. And I hated myself for being too scared to bash the guy's head in. And I hated myself for not being enough for my mom, 'cause she always needed a guy, and that guy was never me.

After my nuts stop hurting I wait another hour in my room before my mom's car rumbles into the parking lot. Finally! I head to the kitchen. On the top shelf of the fridge are two big pots. Rice and black beans. In an old margarine tub there's day-old mac and cheese. Half an onion chills by its lonesome in the bottom see-through drawer.

The second shelf's off-limits. There Brian has four cans of Natural Ice, half a tube of ground beef, his two liter of

Pepsi, and the sausage he eats with generic Ritz.

Brian's latest thing is writing down my chores for the day. Here's the list pinned to the fridge with a magnet, the Pizza Hut hotline we never call.

Today I had to sweep and mop the kitchen, dust everywhere in the house. Yesterday I had to vacuum and clean the whole bathroom, scrub the toilet, sink, tub, and all. He shook the can of Comet before and after to make sure I didn't use too much.

I serve the mac and cheese on a plate and add a raw *plátano* on the side, stabbed three times with a fork. I'm returning the onion to the bottom drawer when Brian comes in.

"You own Teco Electric now?"

"No."

"You must have buddies at Teco that you can just call up and say, 'Don't send a bill this month.'"

"I was putting something back," I tell him.

"You're the big shot who can leave the fridge door open all day." He puts two fingers on my forehead and pushes me aside.

I put the plate in the microwave, secure the door closed with the piece of carton, folded four times, that we use to keep it shut.

Brian stands in front of the open fridge chugging from his bottle of Pepsi. He caps it and makes a new mark with the black Sharpie, a tiny dash over the logo. If the cheap bastard finds the level of the soda lower than marked, he'll kick my ass. I take his word for it, don't even touch the bottle. He puts his nasty lips on it anyway.

Leaving the kitchen, Brian bumps his shoulder into my head and I catch myself on the counter. Was that a one-time thing or is this bumping here to say?

The microwave zooms as the plate turns in the light. Just before the beep, the front door opens.

My mom says hi to Brian, then to me, while heading to her bedroom.

Just like with my grandma, I used to greet my mom with the typical *Bendición*, and she'd hit me back with *Que Dios te bendiga*, a habit we ditched when Brian moved in. He said he didn't like that Spanish bullshit. Paranoid fucker probably thought we was talking about him.

My grandma ain't around anymore, so now I don't say *Bendición* to her either. We didn't see her much anyway, and only spent one Thanksgiving with her.

For me, Thanksgiving means eating at Obie's or Jason's with the sometimes lie that my mom's at work. Except that we got a special call one day, my grandma inviting us to dinner.

Hours later my mom rolled her eyes at my nice white button-up and told me it wasn't that sorta Thanksgiving. She was right. No red goopy sauce like at Jason's. No sweet potato pie like at Obie's. On the table was the same food my grandma served any time I saw her. Arroz con gandules, black beans, yucca with garlic sauce, and then came the surprise dish—thin fried steaks with sliced tomato. She let me admire everything before saying, *I no cook turkeys.*

As me and my mom took our plates to the couch, my grandma asked us to join her at the table. My mom said something like, *So we're a family now?*

The yelling match popped off, my Spanish too weak to follow it. I wanted to feel bad for my grandma 'cause I'd gotten yelled at millions of times, knew how much it sucked, but she wasn't my favorite person. Though my grandma never spanked me like my mom, she bossed me around and was the queen of yelling. When I didn't close the door super quick, letting the cool air escape, she yelled so loud the neighbor's dog barked.

Anyway, my grandma's eyes was misting up behind her thick glasses. Watching her, the way she took small bites, the slow chewing, I wanted to cry too.

But then the weirdest thing happened. I got happy. I thought, why would she be all heartsick crying if she didn't love my mom? And if she loved my mom then maybe she loved me.

So it was a nice Thanksgiving, just us three, no boyfriend around, until another fight got so ugly we left the table and the apartment before dessert. Before—get this— the pumpkin pie!

My grandma actually bought a pumpkin pie somewhere. My mom don't touch desserts, and sweets at my grandma's meant bananas or sugar for her coffee. Did she think about me and buy a pie? Sometimes small things mean big things.

Not that I believe in heaven for sure, but if one day I run into my grandma on some cloud up there, I'll ask, *Did pumpkin pie mean love?*

"Mom," I say now. "Wait up."

I reach her in the short hallway, just before her bedroom door. I pull out the Future Success pamphlet from my back pocket and hand it to her.

She's never gone to anything 'cause of me but I'm trying to be hopeful. Like maybe I can work on her, bit by bit, and with the baseball game six weeks away I got time. There at the stadium, other kids with their moms, she might see how families are supposed to be. All about talking and sharing and smiling. Not silence and distance.

"I got chosen for this," I tell her. "It's a program for kids who teachers think are smart but ain't getting good grades."

As she reads the cover of the pamphlet, which explains the same thing, she looks more bored than usual, ready to fall asleep standing up.

"It's a really good class and they're having this parent/student day in six weeks."

I tell her about what we learning in class, sounding excited 'cause I want her to catch some excitement. I want her to be proud of me for getting in the class. I want her to ask me about it every week and about school in general. I want her to push me, the way she's always pushed me to do the dishes, clean the bathroom, and do all my other chores.

"There will be a free bus ride, and free food at the stadium," I say, using my happy voice. "It's a one-time thing, the only high school event you'll ever gotta do, forget graduation." I'm speaking super fast, never pausing so she can't say no. "Plus the seats are good," I add, as if I know or it matters.

As I'm getting to the end, about how we'll get home early, I run outta breath. She's shaking her head. "I'm not into sports, Marcos."

That ain't breaking news. She never went to my basketball games at the Boys Club.

"Brian likes baseball," she says. "Ask him."

Shoulda known she'd go there. Brian *loves* baseball, and the Rays sure are his team. He watches with his cap on, screaming at the TV whenever they mess up.

If I can't convince my mom, at least I got time to find someone else.

She glances at her watch. Her *telenovela* will be on soon.

"You got a few weeks to think about it," I say, but she's already closing the door.

13

THE TWO-floor apartment building on Ecken Street is wedged between its parking lot on one side and a loud used tire shop on the other. Somewhere in there, inside the walls of beige patches over older brown paint, is Amy. Stairs slant down from the small balconies to meet the broken sidewalk. Only a few of the towering lamps work, so as I make my way between rows of cars my eyes are working mostly in the dark.

I'd be embarrassed to invite any girl to Maesta, and here Amy's place looks almost as bad, the cars just as old and ugly, the stucco walls tagged.

She told me I'd recognize her window but gave me no clues. I pass a brightly lit living room, two shirtless boys wrestling in there, then pass a Confederate flag in the window.

Punk music's coming from deep in back. I follow the

chaos of guitar and fast drums until I'm under a black curtain with a hand-bleached anarchy symbol.

After getting on the school computer to look for answers, I'd say this is our first date. Sometimes hanging out's just hanging out. That's what *funchik97* wrote on one of the forums, and she had more than 700 advice points racked up.

I pinch out a few of the tiniest pebbles from between the cracks in the sidewalk. I wait for the silent pause between two songs and then chuck them all at once, hard rain against the glass. When Amy lifts a corner of the curtain, my heart does a flip. Her face in the yellow glow of the window, in the middle of this black night, is the prettiest painting ever made.

She comes out and takes the stairs down quick, which I interpret right away.

(She's eager to hang with me!)

We walk side by side, me pushing my bike. She apologizes 'cause I couldn't go to her door and tells me her stepdad's sorta weird.

"Actually," she says, "he's not weird. He's an asshole."

(Damn. So was she just eager to get away from him?)

I tell Obie stories, not knowing how I got on the topic. Probably 'cause I'm forever worrying about him.

"Black kid your height?" Amy asks. "Always sitting next to you in the cafeteria?"

(She notices me!)

"That's him," I say.

I mention the time we got jumped in the Rent-A-Center parking lot. After the three kids eyed us, then each other, I stopped tying my sneaker to hop on my bike. I pedaled hard, hearing footfalls behind me. My bike skidded and fell. As I tried to pull my pant leg outta the bike chain, the *fift-fift* of sneakers got louder. Obie came back and took a beating with me.

"He coulda left but didn't," I say.

Every time I think or talk about it I wonder, *What if the situation was switched?* And with that thought I miss Obie again.

That happens sometimes, even though I see him every day. Us kicking it ain't what's called "quality time." Not anymore. When he do have time, at school and on the basketball court, there are always other people around.

"I wish I had a best friend," Amy says. "But I don't get along with girls too great."

(She gets along with boys! She wants a boyfriend!)

We cross the grassy field of the high school, where date number zero or one took place. Tall fluorescent lights beam down on us, the grass shimmering bright green.

Up ahead! Fuck! It's the brown mutt who'll ruin everything! It's lying in a triangle of shade cast by the gym. I take the biggest breath I can without making noise and wonder if Amy can hear my heart banging in my chest. Last time Obie scared the dog off, but how am I gonna act like a little bitch in front of Amy?

It notices us, gets up, and trots our way, ears pointing up. I keep pushing my bike, ready to use it as a shield.

"Don't worry," Amy says. "He's cool."

"I know." And part of me sorta does know that.

"It's okay to be scared of dogs, Marcos."

(She likes me so much she ignores my wussiness!)

"I ain't scared," I tell her.

Hunched over, she shuffles up to the dog inch by inch, showing her palms. He does a quick turn, hurries off, then runs back. When he sorta stands still, Amy pets him on the head, which chills him out. He likes that.

She looks over her shoulder to me. "I said it's okay to be scared of dogs, macho man."

I think of home and big muscles and unlit neighborhoods and groups of boys I don't know. "I ain't scared of nothing."

Her hand slides down the dog's spine, ruffling the short fur when it comes back up. His eyes blink slower with every stroke.

"Poor little dude needs love," she says. "Just like everybody else."

(Like me and you!)

Never seen it that way, but he is a poor little dude. Amy's right. This dog needs love, and lucky him that he can get it from anywhere. What a cinch to keep this dog. Just take him home, feed him, and he's part of the family.

Wish we humans could choose our family.

It's a good time, me and Amy kicking it on the field, our conversation all over the place, hitting school and music and the dumb things kids post on the internet. We laughing like we been hanging out forever, and I realize that I ain't been analyzing nothing.

I decide to come clean. "I'm scared of dogs. Don't know why."

She smiles big. After a pause she says, "I'm scared of spiders so let's make a deal. I keep dogs away from you, and you keep spiders away from me."

"Deal."

She gets up and brushes off grass from the back of her pants. "I better go, but we gotta hang out more, Marcos."

(Like couples do!)

It's the perfect time to ask her, so I do. "Do you wanna go to the school play tomorrow night?"

She looks surprised, like maybe school plays are lame, so I add an important detail. "Zach's in it."

"Sure," she says. "Sounds cool. I'll meet you there."

I wanna tap-dance or scream so all this happiness in me don't give me a heart attack or something.

Walking back across the field, the dog trots beside her, tail keeping beat with his paws. Between me and him is my soon-to-be girlfriend and then my bike as an extra shield. I ain't so scared anymore.

Amy stops when we get to the end of the grass.

"These cars out here will squash you," she tells him. "Go!"

"Pretty sure the dog don't understand English."

But after she shouts it again he takes off, no doubt returning to the patch of night in the light-drenched field.

Walking along the dark street I wonder if Amy's on edge like me. She's acting normal. Probably 'cause girls ain't under pressure to make the first move, just wait for it. Is she waiting? Should I hold her hand? Skip that and ask her to be my girlfriend?

Her stepdad might be smoking his after-dinner cigarette outside, she says, so we end up under the two palm trees outside her building. A lightbulb hanging off the roof ledge stretches the skinny palm tree shadows straight across the street.

With her in front of me I'm nervous and got nowhere else good to look. So I turn my eyes up to the sky.

The stars clustered together up there shock me. "Wow," I say.

She also looks up. "Holy shit. They're extra bright tonight."

I remember from Mr. Ramirez's science class that the togetherness up there is just an illusion. That stars are so far apart that the distance is measured by light-years instead of miles.

I notice one dart away from the cluster.

"Check it out," Amy says. "A shooting star."

"Dope."

Sometimes I have these nightmares where I start floating up, from the basketball court, the classroom, or wherever, and nobody notices me going higher and higher through the sky, speeding up out of view, faster all the time until I'm rocketing through space in a blinding white light. There's no wall or net to stop me, no border where outer space ends.

It scares me so much I wake up in a sweat, feeling my heart beat through my whole body.

Now I look at Amy and ask, "Do you ever get so lonely that it's like you're blinded by white light and your heart's about to burst?"

Did I really just say that? I feel my cheeks get hot from embarrassment. That was crazy weird, easily the lamest thing I've ever said.

She says, "I'm lonely most of the time."

What comes outta my mouth next surprises me with how easy it is to say. "Same here. With people around too. It sucks, but I gotta admit that sometimes, for a few seconds, it feels good to be in my room all alone."

"Because it makes sense."

"Exactly," I say, no longer feeling even a little lonely.

"What's going on inside me doesn't match what's going on around me," Amy says. "So when I'm alone it feels right because I'm *literally* alone."

And there it is. She gets me. Like she's already my

girlfriend. Right here it's going down. I know it's the right moment. I'm supposed to kiss her.

The nerves hit me again. Maybe you ain't allowed to kiss a girl until she's your girlfriend. Or do you kiss a girl so she *becomes* your girlfriend? Them two thoughts battle in my head until I notice a man across the street coming this way, taking a puff of a cigarette that is mostly butt.

I take a step back.

Amy turns and stiffens with fear. Our moment has passed.

The man's so round it's a wonder he can walk that fast. My neck sweats. He takes another puff, keeping me locked in sight, and flicks the butt onto the street.

"Go home, Marcos," she says. "Catch you later."

She starts to take off, but then the man's voice booms. "Amy!"

The shout stops her. He's crossing the street, causing a car to slow and honk. He's coming right at us.

Something's different about Amy. She looks breakable and super small, tiny enough to pick up with one hand and carry away. She's one way at school and another way at home. That's what she said in the dugout and I'm seeing it now.

I'm shaking as her stepdad takes the last few steps. He stands between us, looks back and forth, maybe expecting us to keep talking. Then fixes his eyes on me. His bushy blond beard has some gray in it.

Dads ain't supposed to like their daughter's boyfriends and maybe stepdads are no different. For all he knows I *am* her boyfriend. That icy stare he's giving me? It's like he's caught us having sex or something. Talk about injustice. If he's gonna kill me for having sex, at least me and Amy coulda done it, and if not sex then a real kiss and not that quick peck she gave me.

He turns to Amy. "Home. Now."

My spine freezes up.

"Later, Marcos," she says, hurrying away.

Just me and him now. The man, already close, steps closer. Though he's got only two inches on me, his big roundness makes me feel like a bug, squishable. "A little late to be out, don't you think?"

He says it all helpful, a librarian comment. It ain't even nine.

"I don't know." My voice comes out wavy.

He strokes his beard. "Why're you hanging around Amy?"

"I came by to . . ." What did I come by to do? "She's my . . ." What's the word? Will *friend* get me killed? "I know her, you know, from school and all . . . I just—"

"Pull the burrito out your mouth, amigo. Can't understand a word you're saying."

So he's one of those. Usually it ain't this obvious. You just get a salty stare or else they look away, like you some stinky wacko trying to bum change.

With my boys around, we'd be stomping this guy right now. But with my boys around, Duck Dynasty wouldn't be talking shit.

I get on my bike. "Guess I'll go."

"That right there's a great idea," he says.

I ride away. They only words, and tonight they hurt less than usual. Maybe 'cause I just spent time with awesome Amy, the girl who'll become my girlfriend. Whether that racist piece of shit likes it or not.

14

Hanna High's alive with families tonight. On both sides of the street and in the parking lot they step outta cars and SUVs, sets of relatives, also grandparents, many looking sharp as they head to the auditorium. I bike through the swarm and lock my orange Huffy to the rack.

My boys are watching TV at Jason's or Art's, no idea that I'm at school when I ain't gotta be. On a Saturday night.

It sorta feels like the spring dance, the thrill of the night filling me before I step into the music-filled gym, all them kids outnumbering teachers and chaperones, me and my boys with free run of the halls. Except tonight the thrill's being with Amy.

The plan's to watch the play and then, after walking her home, I'll pop the question.

Will you be my girlfriend? Will you go out with me? I been practicing both in my head and can't make up my mind. *Will you be my girlfriend?* sounds super fancy, something you say down on one knee while holding flowers or a shiny ring. But what if I ask *Will you go out with me?* and she answers *Where?*

In the auditorium lobby I wait on a bench to watch the steady flow of people.

Mr. Davis, my English teacher and the director of the play, is smile-nodding at every person entering the auditorium. Happy like there's admission and it's making his pockets fat.

Some kids unattached to families come in twos or threes, mostly juniors and seniors. A few groups are double that.

On the other side of the glass door is the happiest family you've ever seen, the father suited up, an arm around a hot lady, their two little kids with new clothes like yesterday was their birthday.

Then I see Amy's face between two sets of grown-up shoulders, her lips moving. Talking to someone next to her. I catch sight of some punked-out kid, the sides of his head shaved, the top part buzzed army-short. The room goes wobbly.

Who's *that* chump? He's skinny like me. Wonder if I can take him.

Why do I wonder that? It ain't like I'd fight him anyway. And so what if she's with him? It could be a friend.

Girls have guy friends. It could totally be a friend.

He looks older. Could it be a brother?

They come into the lobby, share a glance that says, *Yep, that's Marcos*, and something about how their eyes meet, the way they walking, tells me he's a boyfriend for sure.

"Marcos!" Amy's face brightens. "There you are!"

Like it's the happiest she's ever been while this is the most crushed I've ever felt. This girl I loved thirty seconds ago I now hate. I really do.

"Hey" is all I can get out.

I get up and give her a hug like the world's perfect. I look at Punkboy who's an inch taller than me. Skinny arms but thicker than mine. Older for sure. A senior maybe, but he doesn't go to Hanna. Are mature guys Amy's thing? Here I been worried about my skin color, my hood, my clothes and friends, and maybe I ain't never had a chance 'cause I'm a sophomore.

"Wassup?" He gives me a nod.

Hooray for that. Didn't know if punks slapped hands, rubbed their shaved heads together, or did one of those elaborate handshakes that last ten minutes.

Amy says, "This is my boyfriend, Mike."

"Cool." I go for normal and am pretty sure it comes out that way.

"Let's go," she says to both of us.

I follow them in, feeling like the dumbest third wheel ever. Why don't I just go home? But then she'd know how

I feel. Hurt. Pissed. Plus Zach's in the play.

Brown fold-out chairs line up neatly at a slight curve, some thirty rows, the first five already full. Punkboy points to the center and Amy nods. His hand moves down and without looking she grabs it, closes her fingers over his. They walking hand in hand now, him leading her, leading me, through the tight space between two rows.

This romance damn sure ain't new. I got a hundred questions for her like *How long?* and *Why?*

After we sitting down, Amy in the middle, she tells him about the play—that it's a comedy and our friend Zach's in it. Punkboy's too busy holding her hand to talk and I'd rather shave the sides of my head and both nuts than say a word.

How could I assume Amy was single? And here I wore my new black tee and made sure my hair was right when she prefers idiots with ripped jeans and goofy haircuts.

Mr. Davis walks on the stage and finger taps the microphone twice. The audience chatter slowly dies out. More dads take out their phones and video cameras. There are dozens of miniature Mr. Davises on tiny glowing screens.

He thanks us for coming and talks about how hard they worked on the play. "We" spent three afternoons a week rehearsing, he says. "We" are very happy to present this play.

"We" means him (the teacher) plus the cast and crew members (the students). That *we* sounds sorta nice.

Then I'm thinking of the "we" sitting next to me and I feel the beef flavor ramen noodles I ate an hour ago do a turn in my stomach. Can I make it to the end of this thing without throwing up? Hey, that gives me a great idea! I'll hurl right here in front of Amy's feet and go home sick, the perfect excuse. That's when I notice the *I ♥ M* again, right on the tip of her sneaker. *M* is for Mike, not the band Misfits. She loves that stupid guy.

The room dims and the curtain spreads open. Stage lights shine onto the two people talking up there. I hear and feel the laughter around me as I watch the couch on center stage. Amy's naked on it, legs up, Mike on top banging her. When I try to stop my thoughts they get worse. Amy and Punkboy getting it on in a bunch of positions, the ones I've seen on porn and some new ones my brain's thinking up.

I finally shake those images outta my head.

Then Zach's on the real stage and I'm paying attention to what's really happening. He's hilarious as the neighbor who complains nonstop.

At one point, everybody busting up laughing, Amy turns to see me laughing too. Such a nice moment, our eyes meeting, that I forget we're not here together. Not in the way I wanna be, I mean.

The lights go out to the loudest applause ever. When the stage is lit again, all cast and crew members take a bow. The clapping keeps going, everybody on their feet, the parents raising their cameras even higher. Zach smiles straight at me and I snap outta my sadness for a second to give him a thumbs-up. I wonder if he has any other friends out here, if his mother's cancer kept her from coming.

The applause dies out and I see something horrible. Amy's holding Punkboy's hand with both of hers. Is she trying to push me over the edge?

It worked. I'm outta here. I'm walking sideways down the tight row, feet together, then apart, past Amy—"Where you going?"—past Punkboy, past someone's annoyed family. The rest of the people step back as much as possible, screeching the chairs.

Amy calls for me but I'm hurrying down the empty aisle and outta the building, soon crossing the dark grass to where my bike stands alone on the rack. Dammit! The entrance light's too weak to see my combination lock. As my fingertips try to feel the numbers I'm getting more pissed at the chain, at Punkboy for coming. Pissed at Amy for bringing him.

And why do they make stupid fucking locks with numbers you can't fucking see or feel right?

"Marcos!"

Amy's heading over as the first family comes out. Punkboy's leaning against the wall like he's the auditorium bouncer taking a smoke break. I bust out my otherwise useless cell and shine it on the lock. Snap the 3 in place, then the 8 and 5. My bike lock pops just as she gets here.

"Dude, what's going on?"

She has no idea. All this time she ain't been feeling nothing.

I wrap the chain around the bottom of my seat, telling myself to chill. Get me yelling and I might never stop.

People are really pouring outta the exit now. I get on my bike.

"Where you going?"

"Leave me alone."

"Is something wrong?" she asks, hands on hips.

What's the meanest thing I can say? Nothing comes to mind. "Why'd you bring Punkboy?"

"Mike's my boyfriend. What's wrong with bringing my boyfriend?"

Like she's gotta use that word *twice*. Hate's twisting in my stomach. "Well, how 'bout he's a fucking loser with half his head shaved?"

"Whoa! What's your problem?"

Mad at me when I'm being mad at her. Though it's got me fuming inside I try to speak all calm. "We was supposed to come together."

"What does *that* mean?"

It means, Amy, that we was supposed to hold hands during the play, not you and Punkboy, and right now we supposed to be becoming boyfriend and girlfriend, not fighting while Punkboy watches us like we tonight's second feature.

Except he ain't watching, the punk-rocking, half-bald fuckwad. He's staring off to the side, hands stuffed in his pockets. I wanna kill him for considering this fight too boring to watch.

"Nothing," I say.

I put my foot on the top pedal. She comes to stand next to me as two kids I recognize walk by.

"It's not *nothing*, Marcos." She lays her hand on my shoulder, her metal bracelets chiming in the dark. "Are you mad because I have a boyfriend?"

"Get over yourself."

"That's what this is," she says, her hand still here, amazingly light and warm. "I never told you, but you never said . . . anything, so don't be mad at me. We just started hanging out . . . I had no idea."

Her hand resting on me is so perfect I don't wanna go, but if I don't go right now I might flip out.

She gives my shoulder a soft squeeze. "Please don't be mad."

"I ain't mad. I just didn't know ya had a boyfriend."

"Sometimes I don't know I have one either. He only calls me when he wants."

"Why ya want that fucking loser to call you?"

"Watch it!" Her hand's gone. "Mike did nothing to you."

"Where ya find a guy like that?"

Amy tells me he's a junior at Lindell High. "He wrestles there."

"A punk jock? Are ya fucking serious?"

"We said categories are stupid, remember? Mike's cool."

Everything she's saying hurts, but I know how to make it hurt less. Sometimes you can make the hurt go away. Sometimes it's a cinch.

I look her straight in the eye. "Right! 'Cause you know what cool is. Look at ya."

I check her out from bottom to top—the marked-up Chucks, the shiny black tights, the white Dead Kennedys tank top, then back to her face, now frowning.

"And ya wonder why people stare. Blue hair and vandalized sneakers? What the fuck?" Her face changes. This is working. "Plus your boyfriend looks like the evil kid in them drug-prevention brochures. You two freaks deserve each other."

"Fuck off, Marcos."

It didn't work. I'm supposed to feel better while Amy walks away mad. Instead she's still standing here, watching me. Her lips are trembling. And what's up with her eyes? It's too dark to be sure if . . .

I take off, pedaling so fast I almost run over some kid crossing the grass.

15

THE NEXT week goes by with the same boring classes except I don't clown around, with the same cafeteria lunches except I lose track of what's going on at the table. At home it's the same jittery evenings.

Me and Amy ain't talked. One time we passed in the halls, my heart wiggling in my chest, and she wouldn't even look at me.

Here at Future Success I'm trying to check her out less than before, my head turned a bit and ready to move when she looks back. Which ain't happened yet.

My neutral face is in full effect. Inside I'm raging, one second from hopping up and smashing all the goddamn windows. It's crazy to admit but I wish I could cry like a little kid. As long as nobody saw me I think it'd make me feel better.

This class has me thinking of my future again. Me as a

grown man, alone on my birthday and Christmas. Calling up my boys to drink beers or play, but they spending the day with their girls, with their kids too if they have some.

Breckner has just congratulated someone for reading their weekly objectives and successes out loud. I'm lucky he didn't choose me. I woulda felt bad, listing all the stuff I pretended to do.

But why should I care about Breckner or even this class?

Why am I still here? This class is voluntary. I can get up and leave right now, head to my regular history class, and when the bell rings I go home instead of hanging out at school for another half hour.

But I actually like being here. I was chosen for this and it makes me feel special. Part of me wants to be a good student.

At the end of class Breckner says, "Those of you who haven't turned in your field trip form need to do so next week."

My one reason for going to the baseball game is now the reason to not go. But how can I stay home and let Amy think she hurt me, destroyed my life so completely that I'll change my plans? I tried to bring up the game one more time, but my mom just shook her head.

When Breckner dismisses us I wait for the classroom to empty. It's hard to take your time with no backpack to fill and zip up. After everybody's gone but the teacher, I roll my folder in my fist and head out.

Zach's in the hall, looking sharp in a dark-gray bow tie over a lighter-gray shirt. People gotta be making fun of his clothes but he wears them anyway. Which is pretty dope.

He says, "My weekly objective is to not fall asleep in Future Success."

Though he always cracks me up, right now nothing's funny. I force a smile.

He starts talking about his grandma who's preparing herself for her daughter's death. It's why she does living room yoga, a young DVD lady guiding his grandma into different poses. Zach keeps talking but I ain't sure about what. If Amy used to pop into my brain a million times a day, she's now stuck there, making it impossible to join the real world.

He asks, "So what's up with Amy?"

It's her name that snaps me back into the moment. "Don't know."

"She came with her boyfriend to the play," he says. "I didn't even know she had one."

I suddenly hate him. "Why the fuck would you?"

He don't know Amy as well as I do and I sure as hell didn't know she had a . . . boyfriend. That word pisses me off. Why does she have one and why can't I be it? And why would Zach bring that up, the dumbfuck?

I still don't got him figured out. A theater boy with two girls as best friends. It ain't just drama club that makes me 80 percent sure he ain't crushing on either one of them. All the times I've talked to him about Amy, he never once brought up a girl he liked, or dated, or even thought about more than normal.

I guess it don't matter if Zach's gay but the curiosity gets you.

We walk in silence until we get to the corner where Zach busts a left and I keep straight, past the train tracks and into the last two ugly blocks before I'm home.

Crazy how your legs can move without your brain paying attention.

"I'm out," Zach says.

"Yeah, see ya."

As Zach crosses the street toward the cars for sale, prices on the windshields in white paint, it sinks in that I was mean to my friend. Asking questions wasn't him getting all up in my business. It ain't Zach's fault I fell in love with a dumb punk girl, tried to get with her, and got shot down.

I guess the pain came roaring outta me to hurt him.

And what kind of asshole forgets his friend's mom is dying? And what about Zach's big night on the stage? It came and went without a word from me.

In the middle of the street he waits in traffic to finish crossing. A passing UPS truck ruffles his hair. After the last car hums past I shout, "You was great in that play!"

He whips around. "Hey, thanks!"

"Hilarious! I had to go right away so I couldn't, ya know . . ."

It's the perfect time to cross, both lanes empty, and he looks like he might cross back over to me. "Marcos? Are you okay?"

Why's he asking me how I'm feeling? I can't look at him and I can't look away. It's like trying to avoid direct sunlight that's somehow coming from everywhere. And I can't ignore his question and I can't answer it without being a liar.

"I'm fine," I say, and hurry away.

16

IT'S BEEN five weeks since Amy ripped my heart out and I'm still wondering about my chances at having a girlfriend one day.

I'm not angry with her anymore, but I can't look at her neither. Passing her in the halls, being with her in homeroom and Future Success, I keep my head turned and my thoughts on something else.

In algebra I could sometimes finish all the problems during class, turn it in the next day as homework, but I ain't done that lately. For last week's chemistry test I didn't try to make smart guesses. I filled in the multiple choice circles randomly. I've gone from little effort, barely getting by, to zero effort. At this point, my grades gotta be in the negatives.

Basketball helps me out of my sadness, but not as much as working like now. I'm sweeping the Chinese buffet parking lot on a Saturday morning, the sun low and behind a hazy cloud, the only heat from the Florida humidity. I'm getting fast, will probably knock this out under an hour. With ten bucks in my pocket I'll have enough for a haircut, 'cause my hair has grown too much again. The rest I'll save for sneakers.

But it's hard to stay strong, to not reach into my pocket when passing by the discount bakery or when I see the cups of chocolate pudding in the cafeteria.

I won't be needing any money for dates. That's for sure.

Just before 9:00 a.m., I take the half-full garbage bag to Mr. Zeng who takes his time looking out at the parking lot. Last time I think he collected from the gift shop and the hardware store that share the same lot, and just gave me a cut. Oh well. Most parking lots ain't littered and I'm running outta neighborhoods to look for work.

"Nice job," Mr. Zeng says, and gives me a wrinkly ten-dollar bill. I smooth it out as flat as I can, fold it in half, and put it as deep in my front pocket as I can.

The sun is really blazing when I'm riding my bike home and I remember to put on my poker face now that I'll be running into my boys. Even if I wanted to tell them that I miss Amy, they don't know about her.

And I do miss her. For those few weeks, kicking it with her was my favorite thing to do.

Cruising along the Maesta fence I spot something. Is that . . ? Yeah, a new piece on building M, right in front of passing traffic. Taking up the entire space between two front doors. This guy's balls grow bigger all the time. And you know by the color and style that it's the same guy, even without noticing the bottom corner, the hook stabbing the burning ball.

It shows movement, bodies dancing, I think. This guy was in a good mood. It almost puts *me* in a good mood.

I keep riding down the bumpy sidewalk, where grass pokes through the cracks.

They're on Art's porch. Maesta has these tiny slabs of concrete behind the kitchen, barely big enough for two people, so Ruben's leaning against the wall. Kevin's sitting shirtless on a bucket and Art's giving him a fade, the clippers moving up and down. Outta a single speaker Wiz Khalifa's rhymes flow breezily over a wacky beat and my boys are laughing about something. Happy as hell. That's what I gotta pretend to be.

Ruben pushes a button on the speaker and the next track comes on.

"Yo!" Kevin says. "Don't mess with my music."

I slow along the rusty chain-link fence and stop where the wires have come undone from the post. I lock my bike and lift that corner to duck through, the dirt hollowed from so many kids slipping underneath.

"Hook me up too," I say.

Art nods, still eyeing his delicate work. He's been the Maesta barber for almost a month.

Instead of kicking out cash for haircuts, he pulled a Robin Hood at some store and came back with hair clippers. With the help of two mirrors Art did an okay job on his own hair. When his little brother's fade came out perfect, Art got the idea to charge. Then everybody, even older guys, started coming around for a trim.

Right here, on his back porch, Art's barbershop opens any time someone with three bucks knocks on the glass.

The clippers came with a small paintbrush thing that Art's now using to sweep the little hairs from Kevin's face and shoulders.

I tell them all about the new mural but they already seen it.

Kevin, like he's got more than three bills and they larger than ones, slowly counts them onto Art's hand. He disconnects his flash drive. "See y'all later tonight."

In a rush to see Shanice, I bet. Wonder if the rest of my boys see Kevin the way I do, like an inspiration. I mean, if a kid from Maesta is with a girl as fine and cool as Shanice, well then just maybe . . .

Ruben busts out his flash drive, quick to take care of the silence.

Art's cleaning the clippers. "None of that lame salsa music." With a tinier brush he's getting at the hairs between the metal teeth.

Ruben sucks his teeth. "Ya know I don't be listening to that."

Art sings, *"Ay mami, ay mami mami,"* and does a three-step motion, forward and back in a straight line, hips popping. Sorta passing for a salsa dancer, the bastard.

Ruben plugs in his flash drive. "Some classics for you bitches."

A press of the button pushes Mobb Deep through the speakers, the piano and slow beat of a Havoc instrumental, nineties stuff, and Ruben bumps fists with me for recognizing it right off.

I take off my shirt and lay it gently on the grass to let the sun dry the sweat. I look down at my chest and stomach, get a good look at my arms too. Though I'm up to forty push-ups a day I don't notice much difference.

Art says, "I should charge double for cutting white people hair."

I sit on the upside-down bucket. "Who's white?"

"For a barber, they two types of hair," Art says. "Like mine, and not like mine. You got whiteboy hair."

"Or ya can be like me." Ruben pats his Cuban curls. "Perfect hair."

Art slides on a number two guard and asks, "Why ya ain't been balling?"

I shrug.

"He's nerding out at them smart-boy meetings," Ruben says.

"Double-check that thing," I tell Art.

He pushes on the guard. It don't budge. "Cool?"

I'm still sorta traumatized from last year's incident at Benny's Barbershop. Benny's nephew got distracted by Monday night football, a Bucs thirty-eight-yard pass, and left a bald patch on top of my head. Benny had to buzz off all my hair, didn't charge me to look Buddhist for a month.

The glass door slides open and Obie comes out with a glass of water. With the other hand he's feeling the new fade Art gave him. Ever since he's been delivering drugs his hair ain't gone fuzzy.

"Make sure Art don't mess me up," I tell him.

"On it."

When his cell plays a quick melody he busts it out and wanders outta earshot. It's a fancy Samsung Galaxy that he hides from his mom. He's become that guy. He's a dealer.

Do I believe that? Obie said he'd make quick money and stop, like his mom did years back, but will he really?

My other boys are suspicious about the money he's making from helping his aunt "clean houses." What Ruben earns from helping his uncle at the Cuban sandwich shop ain't much, and Jason, when he had to work and save for months to buy that new bike.

Then the sports bar owner found out he was too young to be carrying cases of beers and changing kegs. Maybe I should partner up with Jason and try something. Being white ain't convenient here in Maesta, but out there, bringing him on my job hunt might help.

Art starts with my sides, my skull vibrating, and says, "Everybody wanna look sharp for Asha's party tonight."

Party? What party?

Ruben knows. He's rocking his head back and forth with the music, winks at an imaginary girl. Then he starts dancing with her, grinding like a fool.

He stops and straightens up. "Look sharp, Marcos. *No quiero ser el único.* We gotta show these chumps wassup."

I used to feel sorta bad for dumbass Ruben who's forever gaming girls and getting shot down. But I admire him. I really do. He ain't clueless. He just has a lot of heart.

Has it really been a year since Asha's last birthday? And tonight it's going down again? This is exactly what I need to get my mind off Amy.

The party room in Asha's apartment complex was big enough for the hundred kids who showed up. A crazy amount of girls came, some of them from another school, where Asha's cousin and that hot entourage went. Best of all no grown-ups, only Asha's older sister coming through every ten minutes to make sure nobody was drinking. Like that stopped us.

Only one bad thing about it. Weeks of flirting had Art thinking he'd hook up with Asha for sure. At the end of the night though, she was in the back corner making out with another guy.

On our way home nobody said jack, not even a "Sorry, man" or something to cheer Art up.

I really wanted to though. The list of stuff you ain't allowed to say is damn long.

It was an awkward, silent walk home that night until Art picked up a rock the size of a fist. The crash of the truck's windshield musta woke up half the block and a second later the car alarm woke up everybody else. I'm guessing. We didn't stick around to see.

"I had no idea about the party," I say.

"Damn, Marcos, that's all we been talking for days," Ruben says. "You stupid fuck." He gives me a goofy grin.

Forever talking trash at these times, like in class right before the teacher speaks, when you can't get up to punch him on the shoulder.

Obie don't say a word. He'd rather keep quiet about not being able to go out past nine. His mom thinks weekend nights are dangerous. Funny that for Obie the danger's between three and five p.m. on weekdays, the time of his deliveries.

The clippers buzz. Thick clumps of hair tumble over my shoulders and onto the porch.

I see a rip in one of Ruben's black Nikes, right where sole meets leather, half a finger long. I say, "Trying to bite my style?"

He looks down at his kicks and nods like it's the most depressing thing ever. "Your style's so dope." He looks down again. "I'm gonna find me some of that electrical tape for mine, black on black. It'll camouflage it better than yours."

A gunshot rips through the air, coming from the back of Maesta. It's probably somebody shooting up at the sky, showing off. So far this year nobody's gotten shot.

"Asha broke up with her boyfriend," Art says.

I'd give anything for this to be a real barbershop, a mirror right here so I could see the expression on my boy's face. I got a feeling he ain't just about hitting. He might be in love.

Art tells us the clues he's picked up from Asha. Two weeks back, her hand on his arm, she told him about the party, before she told anybody else. Best of all, when Art catches her in the halls, she now gives him a full smile and stops to talk.

Damn good clues, I gotta admit, but I'm thinking back to the barbershop tragedy from last year.

"Focus, bitch."

"Barbers can talk and work." Art flicks a hand at the back of my head.

"Ow. Value the customer."

I go for a blind, backward punch and feel the air rearrange behind me. Art laughs.

Jason comes rounding the building, long-striding, cap nearly covering his eyes.

"Six bucks for white people hair," I tell him.

"Ya paying six bucks?"

Art flicks me again. "See?"

I was right about the new bike. Whiteboy ain't hanging out much no more, rather be off practicing tricks by himself. Even when he's here it's like he ain't totally with us.

Art runs the clippers over the top of my head. "Fuck!" he shouts.

The clippers click off. He steps back.

Obie's eyes open bigger than I've ever seen. He pushes Art aside and takes a step toward me, leaning in for a closer look. "Daaaamn!"

I turn to Ruben and Jason whose mouths have dropped open.

I touch my head, fingers searching for the fuckup. "Art, I'm gonna kill ya!"

"I'm sorry, man. I'm so sorry."

Fuck! I look around for a mirror. Right, 'cause on Art's magical porch a mirror appears whenever you need it.

The party tonight! Double fuck! I'm showing up bald to the party of the year!

I jet inside—"Don't get hair inside my house!"—and into the bathroom. Switch on the light. In the mirror I examine my head from every angle, rub the spot they was staring at. My hair's fine. Better than fine. Besides the sideburns, not yet trimmed, it's the most perfect haircut ever.

I can't help smiling as I jet back outside where the four of them are laughing on the dusty grass—Ruben halfway into the reenactment, the others staggering around from how funny it is. I tackle Art who's cracking up too much to fight back. I punch him hard on the shoulder and get up.

Then I sit on the bucket and wait for him to get professional again.

17

WE ON our way to the party looking our best—fresh haircuts, clean sneakers, least ugly clothes, Art with a new Heat cap, and Ruben rocking his dead father's gold chain. I scrubbed my kicks with an old toothbrush, used Comet for the sides of the soles. The laces I washed by hand and hung outside the window to dry in the sun.

Besides the hole in my left sneaker, still growing bigger, my kicks don't look so old.

We smelling good too. We stopped at Ruben's house to spray on some Montblanc cologne, using the same method. What you do is shoot the mist in front of you and walk through it, so the scent gets all over but not too strong. You do that four times.

Walking outta Maesta, through the last pool of orangey light coming from a streetlamp, we hear, "Yo! Wait up!"

Uppercut raises his hand all excited, like a student with

the right answer, and jogs over to us. Me and my boys ain't ever invited Uppercut nowhere. We try avoiding him, but sometimes he tags along, like now, falling in step without knowing or asking where we going.

"Where you been this week?" Ruben asks him. "Ain't seen you at school."

"Ain't going no more."

Another one bites the dust, as they say. Uppercut looks poorer than usual, his Puerto Rican flag shirt unwashed, the green camouflage shorts clashing bad with it, but I won't worry about him.

I'm getting me a girl tonight, or at least a number. By tomorrow Amy will be a memory.

Hip-hop's thumping inside the party room above the gated pool. On the balcony, Kevin's hugged up with Shanice while two boys are leaning over the rail to see whose gob of spit can stretch down the longest.

We step into the spot like we own it. People turn to us, about sixty kids, most of them from our school and clustered in the corners. A few sophomores. A few from Springview High, where Asha's cousin goes.

A spinning black box fixed to the center of the ceiling beams colored lights onto the empty floor. Nobody ever wants to be the first to dance.

Art leads us through the room like we looking for someone in particular. The walk-around lets everybody know we here—*Yeah, the party can pop off now, you very welcome*—and also to evaluate every girl in the room. We nod at the guys from school, hug the girls we know, me and Ruben kiss the Latinas, and we keep walking. Uppercut moving all hard, like a steamroller with eyes.

Asha spots us and screams. She leaves her group of friends and hurries over, arms spreading just before she gets to Art. Then she quick-hugs the rest of us and says, "Thank you all for coming to my party."

Sometimes kids surprise you with their grown-up behavior.

She grabs Art by the hand and hauls him over to her friends. The other guys go talk to Miguel and them from school. I wanna check out the pool, which has been filthy and unusable for as long as I remember. I look through the back window and down at it, empty except for some trash at the bottom, all of it lit by a disk of yellow light in the deep end. Last year it was full of slimy green water.

Turning from the window I step on something. A kid's shoe.

"Sorry, man."

Gotta be from Springview. He's looking at his black kicks like a stain might show up. Now he gives me the up-and-down to know if messing with me's a good idea. We the same size.

Man, he's got the angry-psychopath look down pat.

I apologize again, turn, and start walking away. That's when I hear, "Watch where the fuck ya walking!"

Not even five minutes here and already problems.

Keep going, Marcos. He knows he can take you and your boys ain't around.

To show I ain't scared I do my easy walk, taking my time.

But maybe this is already a fight! Maybe a sucker punch is coming!

I check behind me. He's standing right where he was. Besides the nice clothes, the silver chain over a clean white tee, he's like somebody I know. The squinty dark stare. The way he stands, head tilted back.

Yeah, he's another Uppercut who lives for fights.

"It was an accident, bro," I say, putting more distance between us.

Three apologies in a row? Plus a *bro* at the end? What's wrong with me? Any of my boys, except maybe Obie, would consider that a pussy move. But go ahead, try acting different. The Uppercuts of the world don't need a good excuse to fight, so you need a good one not to—like you sorry or got more friends.

If only my boys were there.

I join Jason and Ruben on the other side of the room. They can't agree on the hottest girl from Springview and ask my opinion, got it narrowed down to the one in the red skirt and the one in black shorts. A tough call, I gotta admit, and I can't make it. Even here, at a party packed with girls, my mind's on Amy.

But not the same way it used to be. I keep thinking about us two by the bike rack. Me yelling and her just standing there in shock.

The room's really live now, a few people dancing, two guys coming through the arc of balloons over the door. We need one good banger for this to get wild, a new radio joint that Asha will save for later 'cause that girl knows how to throw a party.

We talking to some girls from school when Hardstare crosses the room, a thuggish, stiff-shouldered walk, with his two friends who look annoyed to be alive. His stare holds me until he notices my boys.

Jason asks, "Who's that guy?" He always thinking people are fucking with him for being white. They usually are.

"I stepped on his shoe," I say. Then, like an idiot, "By mistake."

You'd think Ruben heard good news with how fired up he gets. "Then what happened?"

"I said sorry."

The fire fizzles out. "Fuck him."

Which means I shouldn't have done that. Jason's shaking his head.

"Who?" Uppercut's here now, his eyes brightening like someone's handing out iPads. "I'll step to him right now!"

I know he will. And if the guy's five times as tall and all muscles, Uppercut will go fetch a brick or a bat.

Art tells him to relax, that if somebody's gonna step to

him, it'll be Marcos. Then they turn to me, the man of the moment, eyes all, *What ya gonna do?*

That's the difference between me and my boys. Some kid acts hard, my boys act harder. Stupid if you ask me. And you might think I'm a wuss for saying that, and maybe I'm a little bit wussy, but that don't mean it ain't stupid.

I shrug it off. "I ain't worried about that guy."

Which satisfies everybody except Uppercut, who's shaking his head.

Asha's cousin walks up. "Which one of you's wearing all that cologne?"

We pretend we don't know what she's talking about, but our acting ain't gonna win us any Oscars. Too many shrugs. Asha and Tammy come over, lean in to smell us one by one. They howl with laughter like we the most hilarious comedians ever. Back with their friends, they say we smell the same and the others bust up laughing too.

Then it happens. A new song drops. That new banger we already know by heart. The one that starts with a teaser, a light rhythm you can sorta dance to, but it's coming, just wait for it, the sick beat that makes sure nobody stands still. Some people hoot and holler as they bum-rush the dance floor, and the white girl next to me shouts "This is my song!" when the truth is it belongs to all of us.

We getting our swerve on, my boys over here, Asha with her girls, all of us in a big circle but doing our own thing. Soon the circle shrinks with everybody crowding under the spinning dots of light and soon Art and Asha are moving together with the music, her braids swinging like things alive.

Some girls are dancing sexy, music video moves and all, but it don't mean they want to *get* sexy, you know? Vanessa dances that way but wouldn't do anything with Devon when they went out for a month, and Nayeli ain't even had a boyfriend.

Somehow I'm facing one of the Springview girls as I dance. A gold nameplate, *Janessa*, hangs from a thin gold chain. The dark-skinned Puerto Rican who laughed the hardest over our cologne and here she is now, black liquid eyes, killer smile, and even better body.

Got no idea if her in front of me is some mistake, but when the next joint drops she's still here dancing.

Looking down I notice it's too dark to see the hole in my shoe. How perfect is that? Plus she keeps looking at me so we really are dancing together! She likes me!

Janessa stops dancing when a poppy song starts. I don't like it neither. Now's the time. Here's my one chance.

I tell myself that she ain't Amy but I can still talk to her. Come on, Marcos. Say something to keep her here, or don't and hate yourself when she's gone.

I'm a useless ball of nerves at times like this, especially with my boys looking on.

Just as it seems she might step I say, "Ya go to Springview?"

For the first time Janessa looks straight at me. "Yeah."

"How ya know Asha?"

Since she don't hear me, I lean in to ask her again. I catch a whiff of her scent and wonder what it would be like to move a few inches closer and kiss her shiny red lips.

"Her cousin is my best friend."

Another question from me and this becomes a cop interrogation.

Then *she* leans in, blue dots from the lights above sliding over her face and curly hair. "Did ya come last year?"

We talking for real now and she don't do the ants in the pants, the look-away eyes like she rather be somewhere else. We take turns leaning in to hear each other. As Janessa talks about the last party she went to, how there's always so many to choose from, her soft breath tickles my ear.

Here's an actual girl who likes talking to me. It ain't just in my head like Amy, all those hopes and daydreams, worrying for weeks if she'll talk to me. It's already happening. The moment's perfect, except that under these twirling lights, surrounded by dancing, it's the worst place to talk. I'm about to suggest moving somewhere else when I see Hardstare pushing through the swarm of bodies. Shouldering past a girl, shoving a guy outta his way. My heart speeds up. The girl notices him and steps aside.

He's in my face. "Why ya talking to my girl?"

Janessa cuts between us and I let her. She pushes him away. "Maybe we ain't together no more!"

"Oh, it's like *that?*" he asks her.

They got something going on for sure. I take another step back while they argue. It takes just a few seconds to realize Janessa's definitely his girlfriend. She's angry at him and using me to make him jealous.

Not that I can walk away now. That would make me look like a bitch. I stand here, shoulders squared, head up, too tough for words. A regular Chuck Norris. So much of my life's got to do with pretending.

He steps to me again.

"Chill, Ivan!" she shouts over the music.

When he notices something to my left and right, he stiffens and takes a step back. It's my boys, plus the crew from school. About thirty guys against their three. Uppercut tries to step to Hardstare, but Ruben bear-hugs him from behind and drags him back.

I sorta hope Ruben lets go of that tight grip.

Hardstare looks at his two friends for some guidance.

Janessa says, "These are all Asha's friends."

"Who the fuck's Asha?" he says.

"You at her party!"

She's making him feel dumb, which might make him madder. Then she does something worse. Touches the side of her head with two fingers, like *duh*. At least three phones are recording this scene and I don't wanna check around to see how many more.

Hardstare's boys ain't giving him the easy out, the

Come on, man, or the *Forget it*. He's still standing wide and tall, pretending he ain't shook. I *hope* he's pretending.

Eyes on me is the only reason I've ever fought. With kids around, not fighting ain't an option. Bruises go away. Bitch-ass reps don't. Especially with evidence on YouTube.

I step to Hardstare and shove him. "Do something, bitch." I say it with steelier eyes than he's got.

Behind me people shout instructions, *Punch him*, *Fuck him up*, saying my name at the end. With every comment I'm less scared. Don't mean to, but I look left, then right, hoping to see Obie.

"Ya got this," Art tells me.

Asha busts through furious and gets in the kid's face. "Get the fuck out!"

Something we all hear 'cause the music just stopped. If anyone here didn't notice a fight about to go down, they expecting one now, right here under the spinning lights.

Hardstare's a tied-up pit bull. You can almost see the pointy ears and hear the growling.

Asha's sister pushes him hard. "Out!"

When he pushes her back, I run up and punch him in the jaw, all knuckles connecting. He staggers back. Before the tall friend can come at me Jason busts him in the face.

The third kid throws his hands up. "Chill, y'all. Chill the fuck out."

Art tells everybody the same thing as Ruben holds tight to Uppercut.

Hardstare gets up, licking his teeth to check for blood. Nothing. He straightens his shirt and pats his chain before turning to leave. "Let's go, Janessa."

Later that night I'm lying in bed, brain buzzing with what coulda been. I wish I could say Janessa didn't go with him, that she brushed him off and stayed with me, that we danced and talked for hours, at a party so dope that I woulda been all, "Amy *who*?"

Here's what really went down. Art spent the rest of the night hugged up or dancing with Asha. Jason kissed the loud white girl and got her number, did it all on the down low. Ruben chatted up Josefina.

Me, I danced by myself, got Uppercut to loosen up, laughed when a kid named Sammy busted his ass trying a front flip, and took swigs from bottles of St. Ides Berry when one got passed my way. But I wasn't feeling none of it. Really, I was thinking about Amy and how bad I feel for snapping at her. How I miss hanging out with her.

18

NOWHERE TO hide. I'm in the school parking lot with dipshit Brian who, waist up, could pass for one of the Tampa Bay Rays. He's rocking a white and blue jersey with a matching cap. That cap's fine, but the cap plus the shirt makes him (and me 'cause he's with me) look like a total dork.

He's the one that asked to come, actually knocked on my door to say, "So I hear you got some tickets to a game." I wondered for a second if I could tell him no. Then I figured he might like me more after hanging out with me, so all fake-happy I said, "Sure, ya wanna come?"

I'm keeping my eyes open for Zach. I haven't passed him in the halls these last two days, didn't see him at the drama table during lunch, and he ain't with the other kids by the bus. I thought maybe something happened with his mom, but Zach could be home sick. Why am I automatically worried about his mom? Kids get colds and stuff, even in the spring. He could totally be sick.

I'm hoping Amy will show up 'cause she said her mom was a big Rays fan. I need to see her and make things right. Maybe I can learn to like her boyfriend.

Breckner smiles at something Brian tells him and they shake hands. Brian ain't gotta be an asshole all the time. He takes small breaks. I've heard him small talk cashiers and once he discussed carburetor troubles with a neighbor's Cuban boyfriend.

Brian musta mentioned he's my guardian 'cause Breckner's waving me over.

I head to where he's standing by the school bus. "Hi, Mr. Breckner."

"Marcos, I hope you pay attention to the talk in the stadium today. I haven't been able to reach you but I hope somebody else can."

Those words hit me hard and the look he's giving me is worse. I guess he found out my last study reports were bullshit and he's taking it all personal. What does *he* care?

"I've talked to your teachers, and I know you aren't doing any work."

When he walks away I get sad, feel like a total loser.

An old red Ford Ranger pulls in and I see Amy's face in the passenger window gliding past me. Although I've felt broken inside since the night of the play, something more breaks in me every time I see her. There's always something more that can break.

Amy crosses the parking lot with a lighter-haired version of herself. A young aunt? A cousin? She's pretty and beachy in shorts and a tank top, long brown hair ponytailed, and big sunglasses.

Everybody notices the lady, especially Brian. A thirsty look on his face like she's a two-liter bottle of Pepsi.

At least the attention's off me. While the other kids and grown-ups sorta match, me and Brian could be some weird joke.

Amy and the beachy lady walk over to Breckner who's jotting something down on the clipboard. He looks worried, says something I can't make out. I move closer.

Some lady sporting a touristy green visor tells him, "We got enough adults here to chaperone all the kids."

Breckner lowers his checklist and tells her, "It is more than just the supervision. There is information to share with parents, and everyone was given six weeks of anticipation."

I realize that the group of kids is bigger than the group of grown-ups.

Beach Girl says, "It was hard for me to come and it's pro'lly just as hard for the other moms."

A mom? *Amy's* mom? This lady looks even younger than my mom, who people mistake for my sister. Back in the day when I went to the supermarket with her, men would eye us both, doing the math.

That accent's another surprise. Though you can't get deeper south than Florida, in Tampa you don't hear the southern drawl every day. But drive in any direction for a while and you run smack into some redneck town— barefoot racists sitting on their porches, spitting tobacco juice into empty Mountain Dew cans, shotguns or banjos on their laps. At least that's how I imagine them.

And it ain't just crazy white people. Obie, who knows from spending summers close to the Panhandle, told me his uncle can spot a dead squirrel or raccoon in the road and tell how long it's been dead, if it's still okay to eat.

Beach Mom is over with the grown-ups, telling a story I can't make out.

Amy knows I'm here. Proof is she ain't looked my way. As she watches her mom she seems like a kid, innocent. And she *is* innocent. I'm the one who got pissed, who flipped out and said mean things to the nicest girl in the world. Every time I think about it I wanna beat myself up.

Should I go talk to Amy and apologize right now, get it over with? I start to get all nervous and shy, but walk over anyway.

"I'm sorry."

She turns to face me. "You're sorry?" Like making sure she heard right.

"Yeah. For flipping out that day. I'm sorry."

Amy turns away, saying, "Okay, whatever," more

interested in her mom who everybody's laughing with again. You'd swear that lady's the reason everybody came.

"Mom," Amy says. "Come here."

The lady finishes the story to wild laughter before whirling around. "What?" Like a kid in the checkout lane reaching for gum.

Amy's got a put-that-down look. "Come here for a sec."

Walking over to us she puts a cigarette between her lips and searches for a light in her big denim bag, a hand poking around in there. When she notices Amy staring she stops.

"Whoops. Pro'lly not the best place to smoke."

And then it's time to get on the bus.

Under the bright lights of Tropicana Field, the baseball diamond is all straight white lines in clean dirt and perfect grass. You can almost see the individual blades. That's how close we are, filling half a section above third base, about 150 Future Success kids from all over Tampa.

Most of the seats are full and there's a steady roar of fans, sometimes interrupted by announcements or jingles, all of it trapped by the dome above. A crack of the bat creates either cheers or sighs. And sometimes a cheer—fans rising to their feet—turns into a sigh over a foul ball. To the right you can watch the replays on a movie screen.

Vendors move up and down, left to right, slide-walking in front of seated fans, holding trays of Pepsis and hot dogs, straight-ahead eyes like no way they'll spill.

At the bottom of the fourth inning kids are still talking about meeting the two Rays when it was just us, the Future Success kids and our guardians.

After a man in a safari hat and microphone gave a lecture about Future Success, two athletes came to feed us this monkey shit about staying in school. Though they only benchwarmers, the kids wish they'd brought a baseball card for them to sign or an official cap.

Brian even got the black player to sign his jersey and cap.

The boring safari hat guy came back to thank all the parents again for coming. "Future Success is about bringing out a student's best," he said. "Students have fewer behavioral problems and get better grades when they have involved parents, so we couldn't do this without you."

That didn't sound right. If it's true I'm screwed.

Brian now buys two tall plastic cups of beer and hands one behind us, to Amy's mom, whose name is Rose.

"Wow," she says, like it's a new car. "Thanks, man."

That's my mom's money he's using. It could be my sneaker money.

Brian takes a gulp from his third beer. Rose started way earlier with a beer from a concession stand to go with her mustard-drenched hot dog, and later I glimpsed her taking a sneaky swig from a flask, the metal gleaming in the stadium lights.

Brian and Rose talked on the bus about their hometowns and baseball, and the four of us found seats together.

"Want some, Marcos?"

Amy's holding out a box of Cracker Jacks. A peace offering. I hold out my open hand. She tilts the box to shake a cluster onto my palm and I clutch it. Love swirls inside me.

Then I remember Punkboy.

A hard crack of a bat in the seventh inning, the loudest so far, has me on my feet along with the rest of the fans, all of us following the ball over center field. Gloves in the stands go up. A kid no bigger than me catches it, an easy grab, and the stadium trembles with cheers. The dad high-fives him and then puts his arms around the kid. A hug right here in the stadium. On the movie screen too.

Brian has gone for another beer, Rose took off a while ago, and Amy . . . I look around. Where's Amy?

Over by the railing, two moms from another school are going at it. The one standing shouts "It's a free country!" and the one behind says something about her view being blocked. Phones come outta pockets to record it, and here comes a security cop to stop this from getting interesting.

"Marcos!"

I turn. Amy's hurrying down the steps. "Come help me find my mom."

You'd think she lost a gold necklace. She's jetting back up the steps and I'm trying to keep up.

Between two concession stands she stops to face me. "You go that way and I'll go the other. Then wait for me. I gotta check the bathrooms too."

"What's wrong?"

"She was supposed to just go to the bathroom, but that was thirty minutes ago."

"Okay." I take a few steps, then stop and turn. "What if I find her?"

Amy gives this some thought. "Tell her to stay put."

I pass people at concession stands, under pictures of nachos and fries. Not many ladies around. I circle a second time and pass Amy, who's looking super stressed. As we go up one more level, I'm stressing too.

Rounding the level, right across from the bathrooms, I spot Rose on a bench. Brian's beside her and there's a big cup of beer between them. She has trouble sitting up but Brian ain't even close to drunk. I know how many beers it takes and he's only three deep.

Rose lifts the cup, drinks from it, and hands it to Brian. Taking a swig, he lays a hand on her thigh, just above the knee.

She brushes it off like it's something icky and says, "What the fuck, man?" She slides a few inches to the end of the bench.

I make my way toward them. Amy musta seen it all 'cause she comes up on them from behind me, giving Brian the stank eye before standing in front of her mom.

"You can't just disappear like that, Mom."

"Take a chill pill, Amy." She's still wearing sunglasses.

"You're drunk."

Brian's eyes get cartoon-big when they land on me. "Marcos." He gets up quick. "Let's go." After a few steps he turns to me again. There it is, the hateful stare I know, the one that makes me feel like crap.

I stay put. "No."

Is he gonna try something? Let him. I'm gonna be tough. Like life. Like in the movies, the heroes without superpowers. I wanna be tough like Amy is.

It ain't got nothing to do with my mom's honor. I just can't follow orders from that dick anymore.

When Brian makes a grab for me I slap his hand away and shove him. "Fuck off."

Brian stumbles back a step. A black man slows his easy walk, hand gripping a Coke. He's skinny but tall as Brian, standing still to take in the situation. Brian looks at me for another second before taking off.

Amy's struggling to lift her mom who's holding on to

the bench with one hand and pushing Amy away with the other.

"Stop, Amy! I don't need your help."

Amy backs off.

Rose notices me again and smiles. "Hey! It's the funny kid!"

She's referring to the impression of Breckner that I did on the bus. Even Brian laughed.

I feel sorta nosy smack in the middle of this family drama, but I ain't dying to get back to my seat. Plus I gotta stick around for Amy 'cause drunks can be unpredictable.

"Hey, funny kid! Do your impression of that boring teacher."

Amy's still staring. "Mom, listen to me carefully."

"Stop that!" Rose's head drops to an incomplete nod.

"Stop what?"

Rose lifts her head to say, "Stop . . . talking."

The sunglasses have slid down her nose. Standing over her I can make out a bruise under her right eye, a small smudge of purplish black.

"Mom, I'm taking you to the bathroom."

"I can go by myself!"

Amy gives in with a big sigh. From the bench she watches her mom hobble toward the bathroom in front. Future Amy flashes before me. She's taller, not just cute but a real beauty, the edginess softened 'cause Rose ain't her problem no more.

Amy turns to me, a lot going on in her eyes. I feel a tug inside me, and whatever weirdness was between us disappears.

We both got a defective mom and an asshole at home. Only I ain't gotta hunt my mom down when she's drunk. If this was the shit-parents Olympics, girls and boys competing side by side, Amy'd take the gold medal for sure.

"How long has that guy been dating your mom?" Amy asks, cutting through my thoughts.

"She don't date. She moves the guys in right away. He's been around for almost a year, longer than the others, so it's probably for good."

It shocks me how easily I say this.

"He seems like a real charmer."

I nod. I wanna say more, but Amy's the one who needs someone to listen right now. I wanna be that someone.

"Seems as charming as your stepdad," I tell her.

"Yeah." She smiles before her face goes back to normal. Wait, that's not her resting face. It's a poker face. She's learned not to talk about this either.

The bruise under Rose's eye was his handiwork, no doubt. I wonder about Amy. I don't know how to put the question to her, not sure if I should.

"He . . . mess with you?"

She shakes her head. "He usually ignores me. On birthdays, holidays, and stuff we sit at the dinner table and pretend we're a real family. It's disgusting."

She drops the details on her stepdad's jealous rages, the wild accusations aimed at her mom, the threats and fights, the heavy drinking that makes it worse. The cops, she tells me, have come by eight times, the last visit on New Year's. Rose's body slammed against the living room walls, the picture frames and shelves crashing onto the floor, waking up Amy on that night she thought they'd all die.

Minutes later Amy opened her bedroom window and peeked out, saw two cops on her porch. "They wanted to help. Lock him up, you know? But my mom shut the door on them."

The worst part of her story is the way she tells it, like she's reading me the school lunch menu. I remember my life before Brian moved in, and if I close my eyes when feeling hopeful I can picture him gone, but Amy's stepdad has been around since she can remember.

Some people are more used to their lives.

Now it's my turn. I wanna tell it all, let her in on the part of my life only I know about. Can't wait to let this secret loose.

A janitor comes by, keys jangling with every step. I wait for him to pass.

"I've never told nobody this," I begin.

And then I'm talking about my home life. The hours in my bedroom, the way Brian acts, how my mom don't talk . . .

Amy's listening like she needs this as much as me. How come talking about this stuff feels so good? It's a straight-up relief, no other way to put it.

She's looking at me with surprise. "So your mom does nothing?"

I need a few seconds. That's how hard it is to say this. "My mom's useless."

Amy leans back so she's resting against the wall. She sighs. "Grown-ups are pretty useless."

Breckner chooses this moment to head our way clutching a big cardboard box. If only he'd been here a few minutes back. He couldn't have done nothing, but he coulda seen. I want a grown-up to see.

He stops in front of us. "What are you two doing here?"

Instead of keeping cool, me and Amy give each other a keep-cool look. Awkward.

She sits up straight and fires back, "What are *you* doing here?"

Breckner sets the box down. Inside are a bunch of the leftover gift bags we got when we arrived to the stadium. They had a pen and pencil, some stickers, a cap and T-shirt, all with the Future Success logo in case we wanna dress like him.

"Not that it's any of your business, young lady," Breckner says, "but I'm returning supplies."

"Well, no offense, Mr. Breckner, but it's none of your business either."

Breckner starts on how we aren't supposed to leave our sections and look at us sitting here, on a different level.

Amy says, "I get stressed and gotta break away from things for a while."

He gives her a know-it-all smile. "Stressed?"

I'd do the same as Amy, protect my mom.

I say, "Maybe ya don't understand, Mr. Breckner."

"Well, I hope your parents understand when I tell them." He picks up the box and takes off.

Amy brings her legs up to sit cross-legged. "I still like the guy."

Me too. It's easy to like Breckner with so many teachers we hate. We list all of them. Amy puts Mr. Hicks at the top of her list but for me Mr. Kirby's a million times worse. He loves hearing wrong answers, shakes his head all dramatic, and sighs at being the only smart person in the room.

I don't get why people wanna teach if they suck at it and can't stand kids anyway.

"Teachers," she says, like it's a smelly word. "Grown-ups in general."

"Their rules make no sense," I say. "Why can't we leave

the section? What's the big deal?"

We talk about the supposed dangers for us teenagers. She mentions the make-believe villain from the antidrug course, the one who prowls school hallways handing out free meth and molly. We laugh at that. I mention the anti-bullying talks we always getting, though I gotta admit bullies are real.

"But bullies don't mess with me," I say. "School don't scare me none."

Amy goes quiet while figuring something out. Then she raises her head. "The only people who've really hurt me are the grown-ups who are supposed to have my back."

My brain swats this around, considers all the stuff I try to forget.

Then I say, "Same here."

Thinking about this bums me out so much that tears might come. I gotta hold them in.

Think of something else, Marcos.

Obie. I think of Obie and wonder who has his back. His aunt damn sure ain't looking out for him, and his mom has no idea what's going on. If nobody's watching out for him, it's on me to do what's right.

I'm telling him to stop the next time I see him.

Amy sniffles. Outta the corner of my eye I watch her hand move to her face. I don't turn to look. I don't wanna see what she might see on my own face. All I do is put an arm around her and stay quiet.

We sit on the bench, wordless and watching a woman lead a young girl into the bathroom by hand.

After two ladies come out, and another goes in, Rose appears. "Here I am!"

She raises one hand to the doorway's edge to steady herself. Then she makes her way toward us.

19

THE BUS rumbles down the freeway after the game. Brian takes a careful sip of his beer but some dribbles onto his shirt anyway. He brought it along by carrying my Future Success gift bag, the large cup placed carefully inside. As we came up on the security cops, I hoped they'd check his bag and arrest him. Or fine him, whatever. But they didn't.

Brian glances out the window one more time before talking softly, his eyes fixed straight ahead. "Ya didn't see nothing."

Like it matters. Even if I told my mom, why would she believe me? "I saw a lot."

Brian's jaw twitches.

Across the aisle and one seat up, Rose's head rests on her daughter's lap. Any fool can see that Amy gives her mom love, loads of it, and that her mom takes it. The million-dollar question is if Rose ever throws any love back Amy's way. And if it's enough.

Breckner waves me over to the front of the bus. Now what? I walk up, passing everyone else's low conversations, wondering what they about.

Breckner pats the space next to him. "Have a seat."

I do. He asks me to fill him in, wants to know everything I know, and you can tell it ain't gossip he's after. There's worry in his voice.

"Amy's mom was drinking the whole game," I say. Is that snitching? Probably not. He saw that for himself. "Besides that, Mr. Breckner, you saw as much as me."

"Was Amy also drinking?"

"What the? 'Course not."

He pats me on the shoulder. "Okay, okay."

The driver brakes for a second and we jerk forward. The bus horn sounds.

"Amy!" Rose's voice. "Amy, we're not home!"

After a few slurred words I turn and see Rose's head dropping to rest again. All we hear is the bus engine working.

Breckner shakes his head. "Geez. What a life that poor girl must have."

It almost makes me laugh, my innocent teacher shocked into sadness. He has no idea.

When he takes off his boxy glasses to clean them, he looks younger. I picture him at my age, riding shotgun in his mom's minivan on the way to soccer practice, answering questions about school all enthusiastic, choosing between two suggested desserts what he wants that night. Super-small Breckner, a kid who eats no-crust sandwiches and points at rainbows.

Poor guy looks like he also needs a pat on the shoulder. Finally, a teacher who cares. Problem is he can't connect. Not that any of us are even trying to connect with him. Yeah, his head's jammed up his ass, but who's helping him yank it out? Who has Breckner's back?

Done wiping the glasses, he puts them back on and becomes old again. "That's all, Marcos. Thanks."

I'm just about to head back to my seat, but then I don't move. I'm considering something . . . Should I?

"Maybe she ain't the only one with problems," I say. Dammit! How did that slip out? When he gives me a look of pity, I regret speaking even more.

"Is there something you'd like to tell me about home?" He stays put but somehow he feels closer now, like he's all up in my space.

"Life sucks for some people, Mr. Breckner. I guess that's all I'm saying."

"I'm sure it does." He nods.

I almost mention Brian, come super close to opening up for the second time today. Then I think of something else. "Ya know why Zach ain't here?"

"No."

"His mom is dying. She might be dead already."

With the way Breckner's face just hangs there you'd think I slapped him. I think back to the time I gave him the finger. I remember some of what I'd wanted to say.

You ain't supposed to teach teachers anything, but if he don't want me bullshitting him, he ain't bullshitting *me*.

"You don't got us figured out. Nobody does. *We* don't even got us figured out. So maybe you could stop talking to us like we lazy and got it easy? Maybe we suck at school 'cause life sucks for us." I don't say it mean at all. I say it nice.

He takes his time nodding and considering what I said. "You're right, Marcos. Of course you're right."

I'm *right*? Did a grown-up just say that?

He asks, "Is everything okay, Marcos?"

"I don't know."

He turns to me, expecting more. "Just know you can talk to me about anything. Alright?"

For some reason I believe him. "Sure."

We having a conversation for the first time. Before now it was just him, the knower, passing on the knowledge. Now we taking turns talking and listening.

"Not just about school," he adds. "About anything."

It's more than nice of him to say that. Maybe this is gonna sound crazy, 'cause you supposed to respect mean-ness instead of niceness, but I respect Breckner right now. More than ever.

I stare through the big windshield and try not to think

THE CLOSEST I'VE COME

of me alone with Brian. The beautiful night helps, the Gulf of Mexico glistening on both sides of the highway and there, in the distance, blurry dots sparkle from Tampa buildings.

I could get up now but I want what just happened to sink in for me. And I want it to sink in for Breckner too.

"Listen, Marcos," Breckner says, talking in a softer voice. "Perhaps you have problems at home, and perhaps school seems trivial in light of those problems. Kids work hard when supportive grown-ups encourage them. But I want you to know something. It doesn't have to be that way."

I nod.

"Your teachers and parents not caring doesn't mean you shouldn't care. In fact, it means you should care more."

I think about what that means. It's like balling with fewer teammates, I guess. The harder it is to win, the harder you play. I got no mom on my team, no dad to get up off the bench to help out. It's on me to do good in life, and school is the one good thing in my life. My only ticket outta Maesta.

How weird that I *do* care more at this moment. It's got something to do with Breckner caring, which sorta goes against what he said.

"Thanks, Mr. Breckner," I say.

I get up, walk slowly to the back of the bus, my heart pounding, and take my seat next to Brian.

He nods like he's plotting revenge. "When we get home," he says, and downs the rest of the beer in one gulp.

I wanna be fearless. I got another three years before I can live freely. Until then, there'll be more disses and humiliations, more chokings and punches. No choice there. But I get to choose if I'll be afraid or not.

I take a deep breath and turn to him, already trembling. "When we get home? Ya didn't complete the sentence, dip-shit."

Brian's jaw clenches and pictures flash in my head. Me dead from strangulation. Me lying in a coffin. My mom acting sad at the funeral.

Brian's voice lowers to a whisper. "Listen, you little—"

"Just complete the sentence, dipshit. When we get home . . . ," I say, my heart thumping. "How about 'When we get home I'll drink more beer'? Or 'When we get home I'll bake some cupcakes'?"

The bus pulls into the school parking lot and hisses to a stop. Above us the lights snap on, shining yellow through-out.

"Just wait 'til we get home," he says.

Rock music's blasting in Brian's Hyundai, the tiny speakers rattling in the doors as we head to Maesta. Back in the day, before rust chipped off over the wheels, a teenage girl mighta considered this green hatchback a cute ride.

I'm trying to keep my mind busy, thinking about the car and music, looking at the buildings we pass, thinking about anything except what's gonna happen to me at home.

Brian turned up the stereo as soon as the car cranked and it's been playing loud ever since, an actual rock CD from the nineties—Soundgarden. Both of his hands grip the steering wheel and not one word outta his mouth yet, which is freaking me out. Hardly a car out tonight as Brian drives down the streets, probably thinking about all sorts of ways to bring pain to me when we get home.

If I was a punkass snitch I coulda called the cops a long time ago. What should I do instead? Don't know, but Brian ain't gonna touch me. Not tonight.

Nah, scratch that. Never again. Tonight I crash with one of my boys. Tomorrow I figure out my next move.

While swinging a left into Maesta, the music still blasting, Brian don't slow down and I bounce against the door. We pass the older guys by the thumping blue Mazda who turn to watch us when a guitar solo cuts through their hip-hop.

Art and Jason are practicing shots from the bottom corner of the court, the only spot to see the hoop this late, a little light from building J angling onto it. They smile at the craziness of me rocking out with Brian.

Smiling 'cause they got no idea, but that's gonna change.

Brian turns his head to give me a murderer look. It scares me so much that I know tonight I'm gonna tell my boys about Brian. I gotta look out for me. That no-snitching rule seems really stupid right now.

Brian parks in front of our door. Before he kills the engine I hop out and head to the court.

"Where ya think you're going?" he asks. I keep moving. After a few more steps his voice shoots down the parking lot. "Get your ass over here!"

I make a run for the court. Then I turn my head to see Brian trailing behind. That's when I slip, my hands catching my fall some before my chest slams against the asphalt.

I hop up and try to pick up speed again, arms pumping, but my T-shirt yanks me back. Brian's got me. I shout "Help!" once before his hand covers my mouth. His other arm lifts me kicking the air. He squeezes tighter, breathing heavy as he muscles me forward. He's taking me home.

My mom's standing in the doorway. "What's going on?"

"Fucking move," he says, outta breath.

Brian carries me onto the porch and shoves me in the house. I tumble on the living room floor, one hand slowing my fall before my hip thuds. I get up with some trouble, pull the cell outta my pocket, and dial the three numbers. As Brian closes the door I wait for a voice. I try to run off but my right leg can barely move.

"9-1-1, what's your emergency?"

Brian rushes at me. That's when I throw the phone at him and hear my mom shout, "No!"

20

"**DON'T TOUCH** your face," a voice says.

A blazing brightness from the ceiling makes my eyes go tight. My head throbs. When I reach up to rub my eyes someone grabs my hands.

"Don't," the same voice says. It's my mom.

As the light messes with my vision I spot another bed in the room and what looks like a file cabinet. I'm in the hospital.

A blurry cop walks in. "Marcos, I'm Officer Clemins."

The big man comes into focus. He's tall, muscled under the fatness, like a retired football player who now eats at buffets. I wonder if he was there, at my house. Guy woulda crushed Brian like a bug.

"Just a minute," my mom says.

She's in the chair next to me, her fingers wrapped over mine. Lightly squeezing my fingers. Her hands ain't hot or cold. Ain't sticky or dry. They feel just right. The throbbing in my head calms down.

"Ma'am?" the cop says, taking another step. "You'll have to wait outside."

My hands used to be smaller than hers and one day they'll be bigger. Right now, though, they the same size. The thickness of the fingers and everything.

"Just a minute with my son, please," she says, turning to me. "Marcos, you're going to answer some questions, but I need you to listen to me."

"Ma'am? I need to speak with Marcos alone."

The cop's standing next to my bed. My mom's got the same face she has on when the car don't start. She gives my hands a final squeeze before letting go.

"I'll be right outside, honey."

Honey? She ain't never called me that before. This could be the start of something new, just me and my mom, no new boyfriend around to mess up our lives.

The cop wants the story straight from me. I'm ready to tell it—that Brian wrestled me into the house, that I threw the phone to protect myself. Don't remember what happened after the swing.

To make sure Brian never comes back to mess with me again, I'm gonna give the cop every detail from the last year. But first I gotta pee.

In the bathroom mirror I look at my face. Damn! My left cheek's puffy, purplish around the bandage. A thin red line has seeped through the white patch. I peel the gauze back and it freaks me out. Six blue stitches over a gash caked with blood. I cover it quick, feeling nothing 'cause that area is numb.

My tongue feels something on the inside of my cheek. I turn it inside out until it feels weird, and see another blue thread—five more stitches. It gets me raging pissed, thinking of payback. Going at Brian's face with a baseball bat.

But he's in jail no doubt, and that's where I'm making sure he stays.

Yeah, I'm telling the cop everything and it won't even feel like snitching. Why should it? I ain't getting somebody in trouble for the hell of it.

Just like Art's little brother wasn't snitching when he told Art about the bully who made him kiss his shoe at school. The next day we came up on the kid walking home and pinned him down, his three friends scattering like roaches when the lights switch on. We threatened to stab the kid in the neck with a pencil if he fucked with Trey again.

The way I'm looking at it, you gotta protect yourself no matter what, and sometimes you need help with that.

Back in the hospital room a nurse comes through with a tray of food. The bed's set up like a comfy recliner. On a table attached to it she places the tray with plain pasta, a chicken thigh, and green beans. There's also a carton of milk and a fruit cup.

"Chew on the right side of your mouth, dear, and don't

eat the oranges, which may irritate your wound."

She tells me the medicine will make me drowsy so I should sleep as much as I can. When she leaves, the cop sits in my mom's chair.

"Go ahead and eat your dinner, Marcos, but I need to ask you some questions, alright?"

Instead of waiting for an answer, he asks me how the incident began.

I start with the part about getting outta Brian's car and I end with the punch. The cop's writing everything down in a little notepad.

He wants to hear about previous incidents. I fill him in on the punches, the body slams, all of it.

How dope to let him in on every detail, knowing I ain't gotta deal with Brian ever again.

When the cop stops scribbling, he says, "Has your mother ever hit you or—"

"No."

He fires more questions, the same ones in different ways, either confused or trying to confuse me, writing maybe one word for every ten I say.

"Has your mother ever witnessed Brian doing any of these things?"

"No."

The easiest lie ever told. He can pull out that revolver and demand the truth with it pointed at my head. Still I'd tell him the same.

"She didn't even know about it," I say.

Though I got questions for the cop, it seems he ain't even close to done. He keeps interviewing and jotting away, fist wiggling. I respond "yes" or "no" or "I already told you."

With the right side of my mouth I'm working on the flavorless chicken and pasta, wondering if I can undo the stitches with all this chewing.

"Marcos, be honest with me." He's looking at me for the first time since the questions started. "Are you trying to protect your mother?"

I take a gulp of milk to help push down the dry chicken. "No, I already told ya."

Rat out my own mom? Yeah, right. I peel the plastic wrap off my fruit cup.

"No oranges," he says. "Don't forget."

I almost laugh at that. A cop looking out for me. When there's a pause in the questions I got some for him.

"Were ya there?"

"No," he says, looking through his notes.

"Do ya know what happened after I got knocked out?"

"Yes."

"What happened?"

He raises his eyes from the notepad. "Your neighbors showed up."

Maesta got my back.

21

THIS MORNING my head don't feel so heavy and the buzz between my ears is less buzzy than yesterday. That's the only way I can describe it, a buzz I feel and sometimes hear.

Dr. Winfield, a robot with a clipboard, told me I needed to rest. With every visit to my room he becomes less human, that fake one-second smile and those dead eyes, so next time I'm expecting him to come in all, "Beep beep boop boop." He said that when Brian punched me and I fell, I hit the back of my head. The robot doctor said something about motor skills and balance, which means my basketball game might suffer, and something about concentration, which could mess me up during all the studying I'll start doing, all that catching up I gotta do.

Nurse Rita hurries in with a tray of food in one hand. "The best resort in Florida, with room service breakfast," she says, rounding the bed and going for the curtain. Each yank of the cord brings in more sunlight. She presents the window with a fancy roll of her hand, like a hostess on a game show. "And a spectacular ocean view."

It's actually a view of the parking lot, but with how happy she is you'd think this *was* the beach, her favorite place to be.

She sets down the tray.

I liked the day nurse Rita as soon as I met her this morning. Her question *¿Cómo te sientes?* I could answer okay, and when we had to switch to English she didn't get annoyed. Other people treat you like some kind of traitor for not knowing good Spanish, like classes were free and you refused to show up.

Breakfast looks great—scrambled eggs, toast, jelly and butter in tiny cups. Apple juice. A banana that's too bright yellow to be ripe.

I switch on the TV with a remote I ain't gotta bang on my leg first. I sit up comfortable, two pillows supporting my back. A sip of the sweet apple juice cools my throat. I could live in this place.

After a shampoo commercial, news comes on about an accident on I-75. Then, just as I'm taking a bite into my sweet, buttery toast, I see a photo of him on TV. It's Brian, no mustache, with hair to his shoulders.

My heart drops. The panic of last night comes back.

I turn the volume up to hear the newslady:

A Tampa man is in Hillsborough County jail after police say he committed assault and battery on his girlfriend's son, a fifteen-year-old boy. The attack took place at their home around nine thirty p.m. Carver Shepard, thirty-six years old, has been the main suspect sought by police in connection with the meth lab explosion in Zephyrhills last November that killed two people.

The arrest report states that Shepard, who has been living under the alias Brian Johnson, hit the boy before neighbors intervened. The boy was taken to the hospital, where he will remain until he recovers from his injuries.

A search of the court records shows Shepard has prior convictions, one for DUI manslaughter and another for grand theft pertaining to a vehicle he purchased from a Broward County auto dealership with a closed bank account.

So Brian is actually "Carver," a career criminal on the run. Hiding out in my house for almost a year!

Did my mom know? What will she say about it now? If she was feeling bad last night, sitting beside my hospital bed, she must feel worse now, but I ain't gonna enjoy it. Now that it's just me and my mom, I'm ready to forget everything, to start fresh.

And it hits me that I'm a celebrity. Sorta. They didn't

mention my name but my boys must know what went down and are probably spreading it around school.

I want more news, more information on Brian. When I find a report on another channel, it shows the same goofy mug shot, gives the same details.

About an hour later Rita drops by again and tells me I can't check outta here until my mom comes, that I'm supposed to stay in bed, but I can wander nearby.

"I gotta keep this hospital thingy on?" I still refuse to call it a gown. This ain't the prom and I'm no girl.

Rita nods like it's bad news for everybody. "Hospital rules."

So all day I'm lying down on the comfy bed. That's how my boys find me, during a *Fresh Prince* rerun. I'm shocked stupid, can't get a word out.

Art and Ruben are smiling. Jason too, though he's got a nickel-sized bruise under an eye. They slapping me on the shoulder like I sunk the winning shot, all "When ya getting out?" and "Do it hurt?"

They tell me Obie will be by later, and I know it's 'cause of his deliveries.

They lean in for a close-up. When I show them under the gauze, they make painful noises, faces bunching up.

An Indian doctor with a dark tie pauses in the doorway to say, "Please keep your voices down."

My boys obey. Ruben even apologizes. Go figure.

"That was close," Ruben says, and peeks in the hall.

"Wait," I said. "Did you guys sneak past reception?"

"More like ran past," Art says.

"More like sprinted past," Jason says.

Art and Jason give me the play-by-play of what went down last night. When Brian grabbed me in the parking lot, they both came running. As they was about to open my front door they heard the "No!" my mom shouted.

Brian punched me once, just like the cop said. Couldn't punch me a second time.

"Punkass didn't know what to do with us coming at him from both sides," Art says. He's punching the air with both fists, trying to demonstrate on Ruben who backs away.

I can see them doing it too, no problem, even if each is half the size of Brian.

Jason points to his left eye. "He nicked me once."

"Wrong side, bitch," Ruben says.

Jason points under the other eye.

"He can see your bruise, idiot."

Art opens his arms wide. "He didn't get me." He turns his face to show me both profiles. "I'm still sexy."

Ruben don't look too excited. "Wish I was there."

I mess with him. "We talking assault and battery, not a Kendrick Lamar concert."

"Ya know what I mean."

Now the others are gonna have at him.

Jason asks, "Why ya wanna see Marcos get hurt?"

"That's messed up," Art says, fake-mad at Ruben. "How about wishing it never happened to Marcos?"

Some jokes just whiz over Ruben's head. "Damn," he says. "I'm just saying what I think. And it's the thought that counts."

We laughing at that when Amy walks in. Total shock.

"Where were you?" Art asks her.

"Walking around." She shows them the plastic hospital bracelet on her wrist. "I swiped one of these when the receptionist went after you guys."

We hear voices in the hall. Amy gets behind the door.

"What's going on here?" Rita wants to know.

A doctor and another nurse come in right behind her and look dead at me, like I smuggled my boys in here.

"We're just leaving," Ruben says.

They take off. It was a five-minute visit, tops.

After the nurse and the doctor leave, Amy comes out from her hiding spot and looks closely at my wound. "Nice face."

I'm smiling so much my stitched cheek tugs. "You too. What're ya doing here?"

"Obie told me to come."

Which makes no sense. I wonder how he knew about her.

"He found me during lunch and told me to meet up with your friends after school. That he'd try to come later."

Amy tells me I'm the trending topic at Hanna High.

She's been reading the news and comments.

"I want a selfie with you so I can be part of the first official photo."

Laughing feels good but also hurts my face.

I show her the stitches, outside and inside my cheek. Tough girl don't squirm at all.

She sits on the chair, feet up on my bed, and talks about how a scar on me wouldn't look too bad. Listening to her soft voice, it's impossible to not think about her in the old way, even though we just got back to being friends. If only Punkboy didn't exist.

"What's up with Mike?"

I damn near say *Punkboy*. I need to stop hating on the guy. He never did nothing to me.

"Mike and I broke up," she says.

"Too bad."

It ain't too bad. It's fucking great.

"I had to break up with him," she says. "I got sick of hanging out on his couch while he smoked weed, played video games and ignored me."

"You did that?"

She shrugs. "It's like if you let people treat you like crap, you start feeling like crap, and then getting treated like crap becomes normal."

"Yeah, I think that happened to me with that asshole."

"Fuck Carver."

"Yeah, fuck him," I say.

Amy tells me how all those kids staring at her and her mom on the bus last night got her to look at life in a new way. "I don't know how to help my mom and I'm sick of feeling guilty about it."

"I hear you. I'm not dealing with my mom once I hit eighteen. I've wanted that asshole outta the house this whole time, but I realized I want to get outta that house too. I want a future out of Maesta. I'm going to college."

I say it like it's a fact and all of a sudden it feels like one.

"Speaking of school," Amy says, and takes out a blue folder from her backpack. "I got the work you gotta make up."

Schoolwork for Marcos is written in neat penmanship. Inside are worksheets from my classes, assignments from teachers. How great is this girl?

In the middle of semester I'm flunking all my classes except PE. The thought of repeating my sophomore year scares the hell outta me. All day I been worried about the work I was missing, and now that it's in my hands, I know I'll do the assignments. Breckner's words still got me caring.

Amy says we should study together, and I'm down, but since the pills are making me drowsy and slow in the brain I let her do most of the talking.

She tells me how Obie found her behind the gym and invited her to the hospital. How player Ruben joke-flirted with her nonstop, how Jason paid his bus fare with nickels and dimes, how Art stood up to give Amy his seat when she gave hers to an old man.

She talks about herself too, but don't say nothing half as interesting as when she said "Mike and I broke up."

22

AFTER KNOCKING out the ten algebra problems and studying the periodic table for chemistry, I see that it's just past five, about an hour since Amy left.

That's a long time for me to sit still, especially if I'm doing schoolwork, so I'm happy when the beige phone in my room rings. A nurse came by earlier to say my mom would pick me up at seven, and that my mom said not to eat, which means she has something special in mind.

Maybe she's calling again to say she'll be here sooner.

"Hello?"

"It's me," Obie says. "They won't let me past. Family only."

I tell him the plan. He sits in the waiting area with a view of the hall entrance. That's where I'll be, nodding when the coast is clear.

I hang up and consider my hospital gown again. It looks

like a long shirt, a few sizes too big. No biggie, really. I head down the hall where an old man, hunched over, pushes an older woman in a wheelchair. Nurse Rita pops out of one room, hurries down the hall a few steps, and pops into another.

I gotta walk to the very end of the hall for Obie to see me. From the bench where he's sitting he glances at the receptionist desk a few times. When it's clear he gets up and runs to me.

"Hey! Get back here!"

I hurry to the corner, Obie following me, and make a left. Can't go back to my room where they might look so I'm thinking of a plan, where to go, when I see a sign for stairs. We go through that door and down one flight. The floor below looks the same.

We walk regular so we don't draw attention, passing the rooms with documents on the doors detailing the patient information. We need an empty room.

At a dead end I try the doorknob. It turns. I switch on the light and am so shocked I just stand there for a few seconds before closing the door.

An operating room. White metal arms come down from the ceiling and turn into big round lamps. Under the lamps is the table where patients get cut open. Other arms hold computer screens and other high-tech stuff.

Obie hops onto the operation table.

I wanna celebrate the escape but there's something bigger on my mind. Still outta breath, I ask, "How'd ya know about Amy?"

He does his silent laugh, eyes closed and head shaking. That Bucs cap cocked carefully to the side, barely gripping his skull, stays put. "Ya mentioned something about a white girl once. Plus in school, when ya look off somewhere, it's always at her."

Which gets me smiling. I press the tape on my cheek so the gauze don't fall off. "I wanted to tell ya. I really did. But then I wasn't sure she could be my girlfriend 'cause how we different and all, but then I found out she ain't so different, but she had a boyfriend so, ya know, whatever, but now she ain't got one."

"Right," he says, not sarcastic at all. He can understand me when I'm amped like this.

He looks different, tired maybe. It's his eyes, dull yet glassy. He got high today.

"Messing with weed ain't us," I tell him. "Delivering or doing it."

He looks surprised, but he don't deny it. "I just smoked a little."

"But you deal a lot."

He says nothing so I continue. "You know that shit always ends bad. You know what happened to Fat Rick, Manrico, and all them."

He smiles at me. "Okay, Mom."

"*Someone's* gotta tell you. Ya gonna fuck around and get busted." I'm pacing, blowing off steam I didn't know I had.

"Listen, man," he says, his eyes following me.

"Fuck that. You were going to be a physicist, remember?"

"What the fuck is wrong with you?" he says. Like *I'm* the one who's acting crazy.

I tell him, "At least one person in our graduating class is gonna be a surgeon. Someone else is gonna be an engineer. Someone else is gonna be a lawyer. You were gonna be a physicist. Now you're a drug dealer."

"What are *you* gonna be?"

"I don't fucking know, but I ain't washing cars or sweeping parking lots for the rest of my life, and I damn sure ain't gonna be a drug dealer like you."

"Fuck this." He hops down. "I don't need this shit."

"You *are* a drug dealer, Obie. Don't get mad at *me* over some real talk."

He takes a deep breath, hops back on the table, and lies there. I wish one of these machines could scan his brain and tell me what he's thinking.

He sits up and says, "When making money suddenly became easy, it took over everything. Became even more important than school, I guess."

"I don't blame you," I tell him. "I get it, even. But you

gotta forget that now and buckle down on school." That's a Breckner phrase.

He laughs. "Buckle down? That punch you took rearranged your brain."

To make him understand it ain't a joke, I say this carefully: "I'm getting outta Maesta."

"Sure," he says, all serious. "Okay."

"No, listen to me. Really listen. Nobody else gets out, but I'm gonna do it, and you supposed to be my inspiration."

"So that's what this is about?" He smiles. "For a second I thought you was worried about me."

I shrug. "There's that too."

He tells me he worries about getting caught all the time and that he got his first C plus last week in history.

He hops off the table. "You right. If I don't stop, something's gonna stop me. Soon as my aunt finds somebody else, I'm out."

"Promise?" I slowly raise my fist.

"Depends," he says. "Do *you* promise to let us know when someone fucks with ya?"

"Promise."

After we bump fists, Obie says, "When they let out Brian or Carver or whoever, he better hope I don't run into his punkass."

A smile grows on my face, so big that one side of my gauze pops off and flaps there like a broken screen door. I smooth it back over the stitches.

Obie's comment is like Ruben saying "Wish I was there."

I ain't into violence, have had enough of it, believe me, but there's something crazy beautiful about a friend wanting to hurt the person who's hurt you.

23

THAT NIGHT when me and my mom get back from the hospital she puts a lasagna in the oven, the special-occasion dish for new boyfriends or for when her cousin Zenaida visits from Puerto Rico.

Lasagna might be the closest thing I'll get to "Sorry," since she ain't mentioned the asshole boyfriend who used to live here yet.

I'll take it. Eating a nice dinner together is just one change of many I feel coming. The obvious change is the house, cleaner and more organized than it was yesterday. The table, forever cluttered with coupons and bills, is almost clear. The ashtray on the windowsill is gone, though the stink of tobacco still clings to the air.

You can smell the boyfriends for days after they leave, like the sweat and car grease of José the mechanic, the spicy Cajun stench of Rogelio, who managed Popeyes.

Though my mom usually comes home sluggish, tonight she's moving like a woman on a mission. From the living room armchair, still drowsy on pills, I watch the Heat game as she works in the kitchen.

There's no Brian demanding things. No listening out for his car so I can turn off the TV and rush to my room before he walks in.

I'm feeling different too, proud and happy like I just killed it out on the court. I guess I did kill it today, with my homework.

After a three-pointer gives the Heat a lead, I hear the oven door shriek open and my mom say, "Please set the table, honey."

The table? My heart drops and wiggles in my gut. I turn off the TV, all my excitement draining away. A new boyfriend already?

In the kitchen my mom's peeling a cucumber. She's got this way of holding a cucumber in her hand, turning it with her thumb, the peeler swiping down quick so that the dark green skin slides off in long pieces. In seconds it gets sliced, each circle the same thickness.

She sways right to let me open the cupboard next to her. I ask, "For how many people?"

Her eyes go wide. "Did you invite someone?"

"No."

Then she must remember what lasagna means. She

dumps the cucumber slices over the lettuce and says, "Just us two."

Music to my ears. We sit down to a family-type dinner, where she looks at me from across the small round table. Ain't gonna lie. It would be a million times better if we had a family-type talk. She speaks only to offer me more salad or lasagna or Materva soda, and I ain't trying to say too much and ruin it.

If she can look at me in this way, like we know each other, it will be enough.

"What did you tell the cop?" she asks me.

"Nothing."

She nods and chews slowly. "What did he ask?"

"He asked me questions about . . ." I rather not say his name. "I didn't tell them anything about you."

"Good. It's nobody's business."

"Right," I say. I get it. She's worried about getting in trouble. "It's all over now."

I take a sip of soda.

"Not yet. A social worker will be coming to talk to you."

"Why?"

"Probably to ask you the same questions, honey."

We eat quietly until her phone rings. She answers it right away. "Hello? . . . Oh, one moment."

She tells me to keep eating and takes the call in her bedroom, the door closed. After a few minutes she comes back. "Sorry about that."

We eat in the quiet glow of the kitchen light with me wondering, just like when I was little, what I can say to get her talking.

I ask her about work: everything is fine.

I ask her where she learned to make lasagna: from the instructions on the pasta box.

I tell her that Future Success is a fun class hoping she'll ask me why. "That's nice," she tells me, and sips from the last can of Natural Ice.

Then something dope happens. When I take the final bite of lasagna and say "Mama mia, datta wasa delichoso," my mom laughs.

Even if it's more like a chuckle or a giggle, whichever's softer, it feels like we really together at the table. And that love is here too.

24

FOR THE past few weeks I've been hitting the books hard, even with my boys knocking on the front door, trying to get me on the court.

I told them from the start that I ain't trying to spend another year as a sophomore, while they get one year closer to graduating.

I gotta pass each class and not just to move up a grade. I gotta dodge summer school too. Maybe that now makes me *ambitious*, a Breckner word.

I still got the ambition for money, and the hole in my sneaker has gotten bigger, but I ain't got much time for job searching with all this school catch-up.

My teachers didn't die of heart attacks when I asked them for extra credit. Instead, they got sorta happy, like they love coming up with assignments on the spot.

Yesterday for English I wrote a thousand words on "The

Chrysanthemums." I was feeling that lady in the story, the one who loves something nobody understands. Then I was feeling the nice man who wanted to fix her pots and pans. But in the end I guess I identified most with the chrysanthemums, them flowers in the middle of the road.

With me kneeling on the floor, my bed turns into a desk full of textbooks, notebooks, and pens. When I'm set up for studying like this I feel in control of my life.

I ain't gotta coach myself like the first days, which was basically my brain bossing my body around. *Sit right there. Read that textbook. You can get up in twenty more minutes.*

I sounded like my own mom should, which might mean I don't need one.

I cross out the assignments from the list when completed and each slash feels like a trophy for my shelf.

I didn't lie in the last study journal entries I turned in to Breckner. I really did all that work—the note-taking in class that made my hand sore, reading entire units again and again, answering the comprehension questions.

I made plans to study with Amy and Zach. Obie wants to study with me as soon as his schedule loosens up. His mom found out about his grades slipping and his punishment is that he comes home directly from school every day to do homework. His aunt found somebody to replace him right away, so I've stopped worrying about him.

Sure, sometimes I wanna take long breaks, wanna burn these books and go outside, but then I think of me and

Amy kicking it during all of June, July, and August.

That girl's damn motivational.

My first days back in school I was given rock star attention. Don't ask me why violence and injuries are cool. All I know's that bruises or cuts get you attention, stitches get you more. Plus everybody heard I got punched by Carver Shepard. I walked through school like Kanye on a red carpet, with kid reporters popping up to get spontaneous interviews.

The stiches got removed and left no mark, so I'm ready to forget the whole thing.

Amy, Zach, and I decide to study at his old house, where he's moved back since his mom died.

When I ran into him in the halls a week after the baseball game, her death was written all over his face.

His grandma's living here too, playing parent, right now trying to calm down his crying sister who just bumped her head against something.

It's shiny floors everywhere except the carpeted bedrooms and office. Through the glass door of the living room I see an inflatable duck floating in the swimming pool. Zach tells us his dad had the pool put in before moving to Massachusetts to live with his girlfriend.

In the hallway are photos of Zach, his sister, and his mom—a lady with bright eyes and almost yellow hair.

I'm trying to act like this ain't the most impressive

house ever. Amy touches the coffee-colored couch so I do too. It's soft and fat like a teddy bear, and the smaller couch and armchair match perfectly with it.

There are two dining rooms, the smaller one inside the kitchen.

Amy catches me smiling. "Fancy place, huh?"

"Yeah." And I smile bigger, knowing that me and her got this in common: our fascination with this kind of life. Zach opens a cupboard. "Want some snacks?"

Bags, boxes, and cans fill four shelves.

I say "pretzels" at the same moment Amy says "chips." I'm about to be the gentleman and go with Amy's choice, but Zach grabs both.

He leads us to where we'll study, his white and brown wingtip shoes clicking on the floor. After studying on my own these last weeks, I'm curious about how group studying works.

We load the big dining room table with two sets of textbooks, notebooks, and plenty to write with.

We practice for the chemistry test. I need to ace that thing, and nobody's tests are harder than Mrs. Kavli's. Even Obie struggles in that class. Obie who's his old self again. Obie who's gonna be a physicist.

Zach is quizzing us. Amy's quicker most of the time, and gets more right. We giving *Jeopardy!* answers. *What is cadmium? What are molecules? What's something I can't fucking remember?*

Mrs. Kavli don't believe in multiple choice. You gotta come up with the answer on your own. If you get it wrong, it's negative points. Even worse, we gotta fill out the periodic table, know all 118 chemical elements and their abbreviations. How am I gonna pull that off?

I'll keep studying. That's how.

I need to remember that every minute of studying will take me a step further away from Maesta.

After we done with chemistry I say, "I ain't never had the test anxiety that Breckner talked about, but I see it happening next week."

"You'll be ready," Amy says.

I ain't so sure. Shoulda been learning this stuff all semester, picking it up bit by bit. Now I'm supposed to cram it all in my head and it ain't fitting.

We start studying history. We get so into the Bill of Rights that I don't even notice the weak light until Zach's grandma comes by to switch on the chandelier. She invites me and Amy to stay for supper. I know from movies that supper is dinner, so I'm all over that.

She insists we call our parents to ask for permission. I make out like I got credit on my phone and fake a quick conversation.

"Hi, Mom . . . I'm fine, thanks, and you? . . . Can I have dinner at Zach's? . . . Yeah, his grandma's really nice . . . Okay, thanks . . . I love you too."

I pocket my cell. "My mom says it's okay."

On the table, Zach's grandma lays out a brick of meat loaf. Then she sets down a shiny white bowl of mashed potatoes, gravy in a tiny pitcher, and another bowl of steamed vegetables—carrots, green broccoli, and white broccoli. After I show that plate who's boss, finishing before anybody else, she offers me more. It's good, especially the mashed potatoes that got lots of butter and pepper.

She knows everything about Future Success and school finishing soon. While she talks, she spoon-slaps more mashed potatoes onto my plate. I guess they ain't gotta save none for tomorrow.

Between forkfuls of meat loaf and potato (I'm mixing them), I tell her about Future Success, my low grades, and how I'm trying to get them up. I answer her questions, sometimes with just a nod or a head shake.

Her interested in me has me all interested in her, wanting to ask questions too. But now Amy's telling her about some science experiment in her class with a solar hot dog cooker.

Do Zach got anyone besides his grandma? Nearby, I mean. I wonder if having just one person's enough. I turn to who could be my one person.

Amy puts a big piece of broccoli in her mouth and chews. Even with her cheeks puffed up she's beautiful.

25

HOME AIN'T a horrible place no more. The dinner drill was always me taking a plate of food to my room or, before Brian, to the living room. Now I can go to the kitchen when I want, fry an egg to go with the rice and beans, and when I need a break from homework I can watch TV on the armchair or laid up on the couch.

After that first day eating at the table, me and my mom have dinner together in front of the TV. She takes her time with every small forkful. Swallows. Takes a drink of her cranberry and vodka, then forks another bit of rice into her mouth.

I remind myself not to scare her away with too much talking. When her fork scrapes the plate, I got a few minutes left before she goes into her bedroom to watch TV by herself. I try to appreciate the hush between us.

A social worker named Erica came by one evening. My

mom was expecting her, answered the door wearing slacks, a nice blouse, and a smile, the friendliest hostess you ever saw. She had Erica sit in the comfy armchair and offered to make coffee.

"You seem like a very nice family," Erica said right away, and explained that she just needed to verify that our house was a safe environment. "I'll have to ask you a few questions."

She asked more than a few. With my mom in her bedroom, Erica asked all the cop questions from the hospital and then some. I musta given her the right answers 'cause Erica never came back.

With the last day of school two weeks away, I'm studying harder than ever and feel a yawn coming when I hear a tap on the window.

"Marcos."

It's Obie. I fling the curtain open and there he is, some light from the parking lot touching him. He's on the narrow strip of dead grass, shouldering his backpack.

"Hold up," I tell him.

It's almost midnight and, after hours of cranberry and vodka, my mom's passed out, but just in case I talk and move quietly.

I'm wiggling the screen. Pushing up top and on the sides. I grip the plastic tab at the bottom and pull. Nothing's working. If some zombie apocalypse was going down out there, the slow-moving dead woulda been on Obie by now.

Obie's shirtless, rocking old Spider-Man pajama pants and Nikes. I finally get the window open, then close and lock it behind him. He drops his backpack on the bed and keeps moving around my small bedroom, sorta pacing between my closet and dresser.

I know what this is about. He's been lying to me this whole time.

In a low whisper he says, "The cops are on me."

I toss my bedsheet over the lampshade to dim the room. It makes the light kinda blue, like we underwater.

I hear a car's engine rumbling. In the crazy maze of Maesta, you never sure where the shouts and sirens come from. During the day, the little noises out there eat each other up, but at night the sounds carry. For sure the rumbling's getting louder. Obie takes a step toward the lamp.

Before he switches it off I whisper, "That'll catch attention."

The engine cuts off. A door opens, then slams shut. A man's singing "Tears of a Clown."

Now there's some sad things known to man,
But ain't too much sadder than . . .

Just Desiree's uncle coming back from a bar.

I steer Obie to the bed and make him sit. Though it

don't calm him, it's probably better for him than the pacing. It's *definitely* better for me.

"I never really stopped delivering," he tells me.

"No shit." Now's not the time to make him feel bad or
stupid so I don't say nothing else.

"I kept telling myself to stop, just one more week, but
it's hard to turn down money."

"So did you deliver to a cop?"

"No." As he tells me what's going on, I jump in only to
remind him to whisper.

He re-upped this afternoon. Then, after bedtime, not
sleepy and a little bored, he sparked some weed up. He was
careful to wait until his mom went to bed, careful to blow
the smoke out the window, but she musta gotten up to use
the bathroom or something. During a second hit the door
opened and his mom's jaw dropped. Then the door closed.

"I thought she was too pissed to talk, you know?"

"Shhh."

"Sorry. And I was worried about what would happen
tomorrow."

His mom didn't go back to bed. She made a call. Minutes later Obie heard the doorbell, then a man say, "Officer
Lymon, sheriff's department."

Obie locked his bedroom door, stuffed his feet in the
Nikes, grabbed the evidence, and went through the bedroom window.

"I ran like hell."

"So ya got the goods?"

He unzips the backpack and holds it upside down. A few weed baggies slip out and tumble on the bed, plus about ten baggies of meth.

"And the joint?"

"Tossed it on my way here."

"Then they can't bust ya. They probably figure you had only that joint you was smoking."

Which chills him out some.

I gather them up. "Ya woulda been fucked. Five fat bags of weed, plus meth."

"Five?" Like it's the first time he's heard that number.

I drop them on the bed.

"It was six!" Obie looks them over. His eyes are on me, on the floor, on the bed again. He checks the backpack, the windowsill, his pockets. "I'm missing my personal stash!"

I wedge the baggies between my winter jacket and a hoodie on the top shelf of my closet.

"Six bags, Marcos. Not five. *Six*."

"You sure?"

After a moment it comes to him and his eyes close from the brain pain of the memory. His stash has enough weed for four or five joints, and it's in his sock and underwear drawer.

He's pacing faster than before. I gotta be extra calm for both of us. I sit on the bed all chill but I know we both thinking the same thing—juvie.

"My mom's a . . . I don't know."

I got a list of words. Too bad you can only trash some-one's mom playing around. Though she used to deal, she likes to pretend she bought that house with her Denny's wages.

Over and over in a whisper Obie says, "I'm fucked," and I tell him, "You'll be okay," feeling like the biggest liar ever.

He ain't buying it. Even if his arms wasn't all trembly you can read the fear on his face. I felt it before he came through the window and now it's getting worse.

I keep saying, "You'll be okay," but he's someplace way far, where them words can't reach.

He starts talking juvie, and for how long. If he can take the final-year exams there, and what if he goes in for a crazy long time? Can he do the rest of high school too?

That's so Obie, tripping about school even at a time like this.

I don't know what to do except keep saying, "You'll be okay."

Again I force him to sit on the bed. Then I sit next to him, my best friend.

He speaks in the softest whisper now, with his last bit of energy. "I'm fucked."

My brain switches to plan mode. I'll help Obie. I'll hide him. Could that work? Brian used to barge in here but my mom ain't never come into my room that I can remember.

Nah, me and Obie gotta run away up north. We gotta get outta Tampa, then outta the state. Wherever Obie decides, I'm with it, no questions asked. He just needs to chill and say the word.

He keeps muttering about no school and no girls. The more he mutters the more I wanna yank him out from where he is. I stop saying, "You'll be okay."

I put my arm around him. Grip his shoulder that's as knobby as mine. He lets me. I'm hugging him sideways, holding on good, like I want him to listen closely. Like he might run away without me if I let go.

I tell him, "We'll be okay."

The muttering stops. He lets out a deep breath. For a while we sit in this way, until he moves his hands to his face.

"So . . . ," I say, letting go. "You want something to eat or drink?"

He shakes his head. I get up anyway to go to the kitchen. He might get thirsty later. I take my time, drop a couple ice cubes before filling the glass and come back. He's lying on the bed, brown eyes shining.

I wonder if that was his first time crying since he was a kid. Me, I've cried right here a few times, and not just when I was little.

I leave the water on the windowsill for him and switch off the light. He scoots to one side to make room so I stretch out next to him. Though neither of us can move a centimeter, our skinny bodies fit perfectly on my small bed.

I figure I should lighten us both up. "Ya know, this is kinda dope if you think about it. But ya gotta think about it in a different way."

After a few beats he giggles. "That I'm an outlaw?"

"Like the Barefoot Bandit. Except you ain't barefoot. You got dope Nikes. Plus ya got me. Ya ain't alone."

I tell him he's smarter than that runaway kid, and that with my help there ain't no stopping us.

"We'll sell the weed and meth," I say. "Buy two Greyhound tickets with the cash and still have a bunch left over."

The thought of traveling the country, hopping from city to city, gets me so amped I'm bursting with plans, listing the small jobs we can do—washing dishes, painting houses, doing yard work. A new city every month, money in our pockets every day.

"Shhh, Marcos."

Right. All my shushing and now watch me be the one to wake up my mom passed out on the other side of that wall.

"Thanks," Obie says, "but you already hooked me up. Figuring the rest out is on me."

He might be right. Anyway, the way he says it, with that tough-teacher voice, means his mind's made up. Then I remember Amy and school and know he's right. I gotta stick around.

When he goes quiet it means his brain's on juvie and what goes down in there. I know 'cause that's all I can think of. Prison bars. Group showers. Him catching beatdowns.

Now what? I figure we need some good memories right about now. I remind him of the time we batted rotten oranges in the empty lot by the hardware store, took turns pitching in a raincoat while the other swung the metal bat, the flimsy skins exploding juice everywhere.

I mention the first time we got drunk sharing a can of Coors Light, how he thought he felt the effect after a minute but the wooziness came during *SNL*, a growl in our stomachs that had us rushing outside to hurl in the bushes.

I tell him our best Halloween story, that year we and our boys all dressed in cheap costumes, us five riding out to Evanwood to go trick-or-treating. How we scored great candy—gum lollipops and mini chocolate bars—and ped-aled home grinning, heavy bags swinging from the bike handlebars.

That's when we hear a knock at the front door.

My body jumps more than Obie's.

"Just chill," I whisper, but he's up, opening the curtain a bit, either to escape the back way or just have a look.

"Don't fuckin' move," a cop says, right outside the window.

26

A WEEK later everybody still wants to hear the details, 'cause it makes no sense for Obie, who's never in trouble, never even messes with the teachers, to get hauled away by cops. At school, people come by like we got something that belongs to them, pressing around to ask the same question—"What happened?"

Someone in Maesta spread the word about Obie's arrest. I told my boys what Obie was into and we keeping the reason secret. We playing dumb. Don't know a single thing, we tell everybody, are as surprised as you. But they ain't buying it. Obie's life is an action movie on a big screen. They walked into the middle of it and wanna catch up on the backstory.

The morning after Obie's arrest I biked to his aunt's place before school with the backpack full of drugs. I went up to the second floor of the apartments and knocked.

Eventually the blinds came up, bounced once before settling above her head. Through the streaky window I saw a shiny pink fabric wrapped around her hair. You'd think with all that drug hustling and staying at home she could afford glass cleaner and have time to use it.

The door opened as much as the chain allowed, her eye appearing in that inch of space. "Obie with you?"

When I opened the backpack for her to see, she unlatched the chain, her body filling the doorway. She grabbed the baggies with both hands and dropped them on the floor. She wouldn't tell me nothing about what they might do to Obie, just said, "Don't worry about Obie. You just forget it. You don't know nothing, okay?"

When I asked about him again she said, "If cops visit me, Cory's gonna visit you."

"Who's Cory?" I asked.

"Ya don't wanna know who Cory is."

So I had to ask Obie's mom. When I knocked on the door, I didn't expect the usual smile and friendliness but I didn't expect what happened either. Even before the door opened all the way she said, "Get off my porch before I call the cops."

I understood right away. To her, *I'm* the bad one. That's how the minds of moms work. Get into trouble and they blame the kids you roll with. Friends are bad influences, the thinking goes. Never mind that Obie's mom used to deal. Never mind that Obie got into this through his own aunt.

There was nothing to do but get back on my bike and leave. As I rode off she shouted after me, "And you ain't seeing him when he gets out of juvenile detention!"

The night of the arrest still haunts me. Obie put his hands up right away, but I still thought the cop would shoot him. I remembered all those black kids killed for nothing, their school pictures on the news. One cop trained a flashlight on him and the other clicked on the cuffs. My mom slept through the whole thing.

"Obie," I said as they were cuffing him, just so he would look at me. I couldn't think of anything else to say.

"Write to me, Marcos," Obie said.

"You have the right to remain silent," the cop reminded him.

"Of course I'll write you," I said.

"I don't wanna lose touch with you or the world out here," he told me, before they dragged him away.

27

THE LAST day of school's always more laid-back than a field trip. The year is winding down and there's the thrill of something new about to pop off. Everybody's got summer on the brain, knows it starts with the 2:50 bell, and though squads still roll together, you feel part of Hanna High. Just a bit.

I mean, no matter how different we are, we've all been through a school year together.

I also feel more connected to the teachers, the nice ones. For the last weeks they've taught and I've learned. I've asked and they've answered. They've given me work that I've done and they've corrected it. School makes more sense now.

I been studying hard between them tough extra-credit assignments, barely got my history summary in on time, but I needed to ace at least two tests so I don't get held back. Today I find out those scores.

On the positive side, I got this whole schooling thing locked up for good. Whether I get held back or not, I'll be paying attention during classes and squeezing in all my homework between jobs, basketball, my friends, and Amy.

My thoughts drift to the summer, all that I'll do with my boys and how we'll miss Obie. Mostly, though, I daydream about Amy, us riding together, me imagining her bike glittery for some reason, us hanging out on a shady park bench, watching movies in my living room when it's too hot. Doing other stuff too because I'm still not over this crush and she don't have a boyfriend no more.

Every Friday before Future Success I need my absentee slip signed and today's no different. I've passed all my other classes so that only leaves history.

Thinking of Ms. J makes my stomach go wobbly, and talking to her will make it worse. Though she can't know who came up with the pranks earlier in the year.

As kids noisy up the halls on their way to the year's last class, Ms. J's reading a fat book at her desk. She closes it when she sees me.

She hands me the signed slip and smiles. "You turned into a real ace student after all, didn't you?"

I feel thrilled and embarrassed at once, like a spotlight's shining down on me. I shrug.

"If you're wondering about your exam, you earned an

A plus. That leaves you with a C minus as your final grade."

Yes! I've passed all my classes! If I could do a backflip, I'd do a million right now.

"Thanks a lot," I tell her.

"Don't thank *me*. You earned it, and I think that's just super." She folds her hands together. I'm turning to go, figuring she probably wants me outta here, when she says, "How did the Future Success program work out?"

"What?"

Why do I say *What?* every time something catches me off guard? I heard what she said, don't need it repeated.

When she asks me again I say, "It was okay."

"I'm glad to hear it. You should have been at the top of my class all semester."

I stiffen from the shock. "Really?"

Of course really. What teacher would joke about that?

"Marcos, I knew you'd make great strides if you applied yourself. I knew you had it in you. It's clear you're intelligent."

The nicest thing ever, those words in my ears. And with that I know she's the one. Ms. J's the teacher who chose me for Future Success. She thinks I got potential. Here's a lady who's got my back.

"Thanks."

I'm hating myself more for pranking her.

Still looking at me she asks, "Don't you know that?"

I shrug. Ain't been called *intelligent* before. I been called the opposite, *stupid* and *dipshit* and all the other names you can think of. Sometimes the nicknames still rattle in my head, in Brian's voice.

"You'll be late for Future Success."

"Thanks a lot," I say again.

I wanna bust out in a song and dance, like those musicals, and wouldn't mind if all these kids in the hall just dropped their backpacks to follow my lead with perfect timing.

Intelligent. That's the word she used. A bigger word than *smart.* Wait. Is *intelligent* smarter than *smart*? An intelligent person should know that. I'll look them up sometime.

Anyway, better than being intelligent, I'm almost a junior. It's a wide-open summer, then two more years of high school, then college, and after college, whatever's next!

28

WHEN I get to Future Success I gotta double-check the number to make sure it's the right classroom. Yeah, 212. The small tables for two are set up like dominoes forming a big square. Kids are sitting wherever they want so I do the same.

When Zach shows up, he laughs before coming over. "It was bound to happen sooner or later," he says, taking a seat next to me. "Breckner's gonna make us hold hands and sing 'Kumbaya.'"

Most of the time Zach's pretty upbeat for someone whose mom just died. When I tell him my good news he gets as happy as me.

Amy shows up in the doorway and takes it all in before heading over. Lately I been watching her close, alert for a secret sadness like you can spot in Zach whenever he goes silent. If she was ever heart-busted over Punkboy, she ain't no more.

Has there ever been a more perfect girl in the world? Perfect for me, anyway. She gets my humor, makes me laugh, and is easy to talk to. With Punkboy outta the way and with how we been hanging out, she must think the same about me.

"Congratulations," she says while taking a seat on my other side.

"How you know I passed?"

"You're smiling." After another look around the room she says, "This is about to get *weeeeird*."

I like the new seating. After staring at the back of kids' heads all semester, it's nice to see their faces, two dozen of them with the same confused expression.

As the tardy bell rings Breckner comes in carrying a canvas hippie bag in each hand. "Hey, people!" He sets the bags down on a table and drops his backpack on a chair.

He separates two tables and slides between them to speak from the middle of the square.

"Today we celebrate the end of the Future Success course and we'll finish at the regular school time. We have a few things to discuss but first, before it melts . . ."

Breckner busts out two tubs and Amy shouts "Yip-pee!" like a little girl. I recognize the ice cream from Jason's birthday parties and the bottom shelf of the supermarket freezer. Tubs with four times the ice cream for half the price.

Breckner don't got cash for the good stuff. Don't get me wrong. It's crazy cool for him to bring what he can, and there ain't no such thing as bad ice cream, but Breckner, if he had more money, woulda bought the stuff that says *premium* or *deluxe*. I really believe that.

While we eating our two scoops of chocolate, curly haired Lisa says, "Thanks, Mr. Breckner. This was very nice of you."

I want to agree with her but I don't want to sound like a dork. But maybe I shouldn't give a damn what anybody thinks.

I say, "Yeah, thanks."

The rest of the class thanks Breckner at the same time like they been practicing for it.

Amy adds, "You're cool."

His face brightens with a happy smile, not the optimistic, cheery one he's usually wearing. Maybe other teachers are the same way. They want to be liked. Extra points if we consider them cool. Double that if the kid who considers you cool is Amy, the super-cool girl of the universe.

Principal Perry shows up. He said he'd be watching me all semester and he wasn't kidding. I don't think I ever walked past him without him noticing.

"I wanted to stop by and congratulate all of you on

completing Future Success. I expect to see you on honor roll next year."

"Okay," I tell him, dead serious.

He smiles at me. "Nice to see you here, Marcos. Nice to see all of you here and not in my office."

All done with the surprises, Breckner gets down to business. He tells us not to forget the study journals, the study methods, and everything else we learned.

The round metal clock shows one minute left of this class. One minute left of school.

I look at everybody in the room and wonder where will we all be after two more years of high school? You can't know, but I think we going places.

Maybe optimism's contagious and Breckner, infected like crazy, has given it to me. But what if the optimists got a point? You can take in all your life, the horrible stuff and the sometimes good, and hold on to just the good stuff. You can stay on a positive kick like Breckner, and like me, 'cause I been doing it for weeks, even with my busted-up face and worry over Obie and my grades.

I mean, if you don't believe tomorrow or next month or next year's gonna be better, you might feel stuck. And that feeling might keep you stuck.

"I expect to see you at the final ceremony," Breckner says.

He told us about it last week, promised us it would be fun.

"If you're not planning to come, I'd like to know your reason right now. Don't worry if your family can't make it. Your classmates and I will be there, and I'll have a surprise for all of you."

"Totally weird," Amy whispers. "Totally called it."

The last bell of the school year rings. "See you at the ceremony!"

Doors fly open. Kids shout and bang up the lockers out there. What are teachers gonna do?

When I step into the hall Ruben's charging at me, giving that victory shout he usually saves for the court. "Yes! Yes! Yes!" I can back up only a step before he slams me against the lockers.

"Yes!" I shout. "Now get up off me."

He does and gives Amy a suave smile. "Sweet thang, you got a name or can I call you mine?"

"Hi, Ruben."

"Hi, Amy." Then, to Zach, "What's good, man?"

Two worlds colliding. Two non-dorks coming from a dorky meeting and you got Ruben, straight outta a reggaeton music video, sunglasses and all. Then you got me. It should weird me out but it don't.

"Hurry up," Ruben tells me.

At least two fights are scheduled in the empty lot a few blocks away. The headliners are the two biggest guys in school, that linebacker with the forehead scar and Puerto

Rican Mike, who I once saw do eight push-ups with one hand.

"I gotta take care of some stuff," I say, and try not to look at Ruben.

"For real?" One eyebrow jumps. "Okay."

Here come Art and Asha down the hall, holding hands as usual. For weeks they been a couple, have hung out during school, stayed seated at the cafeteria together when everybody else up and left, and smiling all lovestruck while the other talked. A couple so perfect even their names sorta match.

"Let's go," Art says, keeping his stride. "They ain't gonna wait for us."

"Hurry," Asha tells us.

Ruben takes off with them.

Me, Amy, and Zach go the other way, through the madness, our first time seen in the halls together. Maybe next year we can do this, even hang during lunch.

The blinds are up in the principal's office. I stop to check out the aquarium and see my favorite fish, the chubby red one. I count the others, fourteen in total, happy that they all made it through the semester too.

When we get outside, Amy asks, "What do you think Breckner's surprise will be?"

I shrug. We turn to Zach for a theory but he's as clue-less as us. He says, "I'll see you at the ceremony, but I want you to know I'm having a pool party for my birthday in August."

"Cool," Amy says. "I'm there."

I picture her taking off her shirt and shorts to reveal a bikini, needing to apply sunblock, and handing me the tube to help her out.

"I'm all over that," I tell Zach.

Zach hurries to find his grandma in the longer-than-usual line of cars pulling up. Me and Amy sit on the stairs, leg to leg, catching stares from people passing.

Except for quick chats in the halls, I haven't really talked to her since the whole Obie thing went down. I tell her about it now and she takes it in with big eyes, head-nodding, and *Oh-my-godd*ing. At one point her cell plays a message-received jingle. It stays in her pocket.

"I'm glad you didn't run away," she says. "I woulda missed you."

Saying that right here, us looking at each other eye to eye. What I want, more than ever, is to kiss her. But not in front of so many people.

Amy asks if I got any celebration planned.

"Nope."

"Tonight we're having a celebration dinner at home." She makes a throw-up face. "My mom, stepdad, and me."

I see skater kid pointing us out to his friends with his chin, the other two leaning in to whisper. Like I could hear them anyway. *Get used to it!* I wanna shout. *Next year you'll see us together every day!*

Amy stretches her legs to the bottom step and crosses them at the ankles. "You ever think about what you'll do when school's all over?"

"Give it a rest, Mr. Breckner."

"The future's coming," she says in a deep voice. "Okay, people? Whether you're ready or not."

She waves to her two metalhead friends passing by before saying, "I don't mean work or anything about making money. I mean everything else, what life you want."

"Right."

"I wanna backpack across the country alone," Amy says. "Just go wherever friendly drivers are heading, hop from town to town. Then do the same in Latin America."

"Sounds cool."

It don't sound cool. Backpacking alone? Ain't that dangerous? Why wouldn't she wanna go with someone else?

"How about you?" she asks.

I gotta stall. What's as cool and dangerous as hitchhiking? My real answer, what I'm forever daydreaming about, will sound boring and cheesy if I say it out loud. Super cheesy if I mention her.

My perfect future's me and Amy living together, in a house surrounded by grass. It's fun weekends, backyard barbecues, quiet weeknights of pizza and orange soda, nice walks in our neighborhood, either along a lake, river, or beach.

Sure, we can travel. We can go to Orlando or Miami, even farther if we got the cash, but home would be the best place ever. All them hours at work I'll be looking forward to home and the girl I love.

"After high school I wanna go to college."

"Me too. But what about after that?"

"I want a quiet life. At least for a while."

And that makes me think of my home, how it is quiet now but still don't seem totally normal.

Amy's eyes are shut, her head resting on her shoulder. She's snoring so loud that a kid pauses on a step to look at us.

"Ha ha," I say. "I'm boring. I get it."

Amy wheezes and smacks her tongue in her mouth a couple times like an old man waking up. Her eyes crack open. Then they close and she's snoring even louder.

She wakes up for real when a kid calls her name. I turn around. He's hovering over us, a kid in a Fall Out Boy tee and a funky blue cap. A lot of kids busted out their caps when the last bell rang. School is over—no more rules.

I recognize him from the hangout spot behind the gym, where Amy and a dozen other kids chill during lunch. They like the Lost-and-Found Club, a bunch of kids who don't fit anywhere else.

"Hey, Brandon," she says, smiling too big. She's damn near glowing at the guy. "This is Marcos," she tells him.

He slaps hands with me and fist bumps, like he's cool. He's totally not cool. Then he takes the last of the steps down and stands in front of Amy, holding his hand out to her. She gives him her hand. After he lifts her up she barely has time to say "See you, Marcos" before they walk away.

29

FOR THE rest of the day and all night I'm hating that Brandon guy but mostly hating myself for not acting sooner. Me and Amy are closer than ever, and she never told me about him. They mighta just started kicking it. It's possible that all I need to do is tell Amy how I feel and that guy's history.

But I don't have credit on my phone to call her.

At 8:03 p.m. I was thinking, *I could go now but I better wait until tomorrow.* During Jimmy Kimmel I was thinking, *Nah, I shoulda done it today but now it's too late.* At 3:26 a.m. I got up to search the medicine shoe box under the bathroom sink for something to help me sleep and found nothing. If Obie was around, I woulda gone to see him in the middle of the night.

Now, with the red numbers on my alarm clock reading 7:13, I yank open the curtain, look up at the strip of sky between the two apartment buildings—purple streaked with pink light—and get the strength to do this.

I hop outta bed with so much energy you'd think I slept twenty hours instead of two.

I brush my teeth, pop a new white-tipped pimple, and wash my face. No messing with my hair. I rock my Heat cap. Leaving the apartment I hear no sound except for my kicks on the concrete, then crunching on the dry grass behind the building. My bike's chained to the water pipe.

The sky has brightened though the sun's still hiding. Somewhere a bird talks, tiny chirps in the morning hush. Early enough in the day Maesta's a peaceful place.

I pedal away from it and into the easy traffic, the air warm and soft on my arms. I cut through the field of the high school, a speedier route that makes my legs work harder, pumping faster to get over the bumpy grass.

By the time I turn into Amy's parking lot the bike grips have gone sweaty in my hands. A lady drives her rumbling Oldsmobile out. Then everything's dead silent.

This is it. I like Amy, and I wanna let her know, once and for all.

Under Amy's bedroom, I see my reflection in the neighbor's window. Something about my cap ain't right. I straighten it. Great, now I'm a Boy Scout. When I pull the bill down lower I become a criminal. Since I didn't come here to snatch Amy's handbag I make the cap a little crooked again.

I pick up the tiniest broken pieces of concrete and toss one at the window, count ten Mississippis, then toss another. I don't wanna scare her.

The parking lot's half full. Old and banged-up cars line the building, and by the Dumpster a small Chevy truck left last century to rust.

I choose a bigger pebble to clink against her window. Then I notice my reflection again. I realize what's wrong. Something this serious needs a touch of class. Shoulda left the cap at home. I take it off now and watch my hair jump up in the window's reflection. So I put it back on.

A corner of the black curtain rises and then drops too quick. I wait for the front door to open.

"Marcos?" Her normal voice sounds like a shout in this parking lot, and I think of her stepdad.

She rushes down the stairs, no shoes or socks, just gray cut-off sweatpants and a big yellow tee. Her hair wild from sleep. She looks beautiful.

"What's going on?" She sounds panicked, like the time her mom went missing.

"I'm fine. I just wanted to talk to you."

"You're fine? What the hell?"

The nerves hit for real. This ain't the right moment. I've shown up crazy early and unannounced, like I'm doing a drug bust. But I can't wuss out now that she's up and annoyed and has just come down the stairs and is standing in front of me all *What the hell?*

"I had to tell ya, Amy. It couldn't wait."

"What is it?"

I shed the fear, doubt, and creeping shyness—all that can hold me back from saying what's gotta be said.

"I think I love you."

"What?" She takes a step back like I showed her a dead baby. "Oh my God, Marcos, we're friends."

I get that twisting in my gut.

Keep calm, Marcos. You can fix this. Just explain things to her.

I remind her of the stadium, of the talk we had, of the hospital visit. I list the times we've hung out since then— the studying at Zach's and in the library, the times I've walked her home. "I feel like, connected with you, Amy. More than I do with anyone else."

Her eyes narrow more and more, like the sunlight's hurting them. "We're friends. Why can't you see that?"

The gut-twisting gets worse.

"Go home, Marcos. This is crazy."

"It ain't crazy." I practically shout that. Please let her stepdad be a heavy sleeper.

"It is! Dude, you woke up at dawn to come over and—"

"Don't call me *dude*."

"—tell me we should be together? That doesn't seem crazy to you?"

"Why you mad?"

"Because this is . . . messed up, okay? Because . . ." Like

the words are hard to get out. "I thought we were friends, you know? Real friends. I don't have that with any girls. Then you come along super cool and I could tell you stuff and we connected—"

"Yeah, I know, but—"

"Let me *finish*. I thought we were becoming best friends. I haven't had that since I was a tiny kid."

"We got that. But we ain't gotta be just friends."

"This whole time you had this . . . what's it called? This ulterior motive. This let's-pretend-we're-friends vibe while you secretly wanted it to be something else."

"It ain't like that."

"What's it like then?" She crosses her arms and waits patiently. She's a lady on the beach with a margarita and two weeks of vacation.

All I can do is repeat myself. "It ain't like that."

Her eyes move skyward. "Fucking shit!"

Loud enough to wake everybody up, but I ain't scared! Come out here, Duck Dynasty! Get dealt with! Right now I'm Hulk strong. And I ain't leaving until I fix this between me and Amy.

Her head lowers. She's looking at the bit of sidewalk between my shoes and her bare feet. "Why's everything in my life bullshit? A fake family and fake friends."

Amy ain't getting it. I gotta make her understand. "Listen, we can—"

"Forget it, Marcos. Just . . . don't."

Her face blank. Nothing to read there. She turns and goes up the steps.

"Come on, Amy." I hear it now. I'm pathetic.

"Go home." She don't turn around. "I mean it. I don't even wanna look at you."

She closes the door behind her and I stand here watching her bedroom window. As I wait for the black curtain to move, that familiar soft pinch gathers behind my eyes. I fight it. I'll just wait for her. She'll appear in the window. She'll see me down here, change her mind, and come back down.

A car cranks and drives outta the parking lot, leaving me alone again. I don't know how long I stand here before the curtain ripples and a gray cat appear on the windowsill, rubbing its gray fur along the glass. It stops, one paw up when it sees me, and looks for a second before hopping off, disappearing.

Like it's disgusted with me too.

30

THE START of summer's happening without me. I ain't hanging out with my boys, ain't balling on the court, ain't biking around in search for what's good. Instead I spend every minute at home, sitting or lying on the couch, with the TV volume low. I doze, eat when I remember, and thumb to another channel whenever I realize what I'm watching and it sucks. My days fill up this way.

The sun's nothing more than a skinny rectangle of light around the shut blinds. Once, on a late afternoon, I took a peek through them.

Now I like to pretend everything out there's on fire, buildings and cars and trees, the whole planet just huge flames licking the sky.

After the first couple of days I heard knocks at the door. At least one of my boys wanted me on the court. I miss hanging with them but I can't let them see me so sad.

And I can't say or do anything to hide the sadness.

I wonder about the ceremony sometimes, what Breckner's surprise was, if Amy was there, if she came dressed fancy. Did she miss me? Maybe she regrets everything and she wanted to tell me that at the Future Success ceremony. Maybe if I get online I'll find messages from her about how . . .

No, Marcos, she wants nothing to do with you.

I miss her though, the way things was before I messed it all up. Hanging out with her as my friend was better than nothing. Actually, it was awesome.

Now everything's shit.

I don't wanna mope around the house like I got a killer flu, but I can't do nothing else. If Obie was here, I might be able to talk all this outta me. Would I though?

Maybe writing to him would help. Fuck. I ain't checked my email since school let out. There was nothing from him then, but by now he musta written. I wonder what those emails say. I wonder what he feels when he logs in and finds nothing from me.

Next time I leave the house, I'm heading to the library to send him the longest message ever.

Hanging out with my mom didn't last long. After the social worker called to say she wouldn't be returning, my mom became more distant. Now she quick-chats me before taking a small bowl of rice, just plain white rice, to her bedroom. The more she drinks the less she eats.

She says a few words when she comes home or before she leaves, but I don't all the way trust them happy *hellos* and *good-byes*. Sorta how she talks to customers in the Walmart checkout line and how the smile, like the blue vest, is part of the job.

She's on her regular cranberry and vodka. Only comes out to hit the bathroom or hit the kitchen for a refill—the fridge door, then freezer door, sucking open and shut. The tiny plop of the single ice cube dropped in a full glass.

I'm lost in the days, can't tell if it's Monday or Saturday. One day I tried doing exercise and quit after six push-ups. I've stopped giving a damn about the everyday rice and beans. Bread with or without jam's all the same.

Days pass this way, then weeks, maybe three or four.

31

I'M NAPPING on the couch on an extra-hot day when I hear the door open. For a few seconds the living room floods with sunlight as my mom heads out to work. Then the door clicks shut, everything gloomy again.

I watch TV long enough to realize it's a soap opera. The hairstyles and fake voices give it away. I look around for the remote. It's out of sight, probably in the cushions, but I stay watching *Days of Our Lives* instead of looking for it.

There's a commercial for a denture adhesive. A commercial for a medical alert bracelet. One for a kitchen gadget that can be all mine for a special low price if I call right now.

The products ain't for me and I know why. Teenage boys ain't supposed to be watching local TV during the day. I need cable, video games, or the internet.

Basketball puts me in a better mood. If only I could make it out to the court. Then I remember my favorite DVD, the one that always cheers me up. I pop in a highlight reel of LeBron James. Even though he left Miami years ago, he's still my guy.

The best plays start with his high school years, already dunking at sixteen. Then it's NBA LeBron, taking the older pros to school. Some plays get stretched out so you can check him out in slow motion, take in every detail of his moves. No choreography here, just the miracle of him handling the ball, twisting his body as he squeezes past two players, spins around others, how he takes flight to make a perfect dunk, doing it all so gracefully that I ain't never going to the ballet.

The video ends. Then the door opens and light bursts through again, leaves just as quickly.

"Hi, honey."

So she wasn't heading to work. It's an off day. She's got a bag from ABC Liquors.

From the kitchen, the fridge sucking open, she says, "Eaten yet?"

Like she cares.

"Yeah." I can't remember if I ate though.

The vodka.

My busted-up Adidas.

My thoughts ping-pong between them two things, and it's making me mad. Worst of all is the darkness of this living room. Sure, it stays gloomy 'cause I keep the blinds down, but it's pissing me off anyway. After the killing sadness of these weeks, I'm glad for a new feeling, even if it's anger.

Who gave me this mom? If I coulda interviewed women for the job, her mixed in with other moms, I never woulda chosen her.

And is that the future me, locked away from the world? On second thought, is that me already?

No way. This is temporary. I ain't spent years like this. Might not even spend many more summer days this way.

Minutes later my mom comes out with the empty glass in her hand, on her way to the kitchen to mix the second drink.

"Mom?"

"Yeah, honey?"

These last couple of months she's been trying for normal and it's starting to sound creepy. Maybe she acts sweet and cuddly 'cause her worried self thinks I might still rat her out to the social worker. Erica left me her card. That could explain all the changes that started in the hospital— the gentle voice, the touchy hands.

I switch off the TV and turn to her. "How much money ya spend every month getting drunk?"

She stops, one step shy of the kitchen. "Excuse me?"

I get up and walk past her to the fridge. I grab the gallon jug of vodka from the top shelf and search it for a price.

THE CLOSEST I'VE COME

"How much is this stuff?"

"Mind your own business," she says, with the hard eyes and a voice I know from months ago. From all my life.

I put the jug back and close the door, standing between her and the fridge. "Ya know I need sneakers and ya buying booze. It's bullshit."

She sets down her glass so hard I'm surprised it don't break. "You watch your mouth!"

"Why? Your dipshit boyfriend never watched his. What's wrong with ya anyway?"

Her face switches to pure craziness, eyes brighter, her mouth a straight line. "Don't talk to me that way! I'm your mother!"

"Since when, *Maria*?" Can't believe I used her real name. "You just the lady who pays the electric bill and sometimes buys groceries."

"*Escúchame bien*," she begins, a finger in my face, 'cause it's Spanish when she gets really angry.

But I ain't hearing it. "We supposed to be a family! Ain't you sad in that stupid room? Don't ya know that you ain't gotta be lonely? That I'm here?"

Her head turns away.

"Don't ya know that I love you? Don't ya fucking see that?"

"Watch your mouth!" She ain't ever been able to stand cussing. "You need to calm down."

I can't calm down. After years of holding it in and

weeks of not talking at all, it's bursting outta me. "I didn't ask you to give birth to me, okay? Being alive wasn't *my* idea! And it don't matter that I was a mistake! I'm here now and ya gotta deal with it!"

Bored as hell she asks, "What do you want from me?" You'd think I been lecturing her for hours.

"For you to act like a mom! I want ya to care! I want ya to open the blinds when it's sunny outside!"

"What are you talking about?"

"The blinds! They been down forever! You supposed to open them! And if I tell ya not to, that I prefer them down, you supposed to open them anyway! Why don't ya ever open the goddamn fucking blinds?"

"Don't cuss at me!"

"You're like some alcoholic zombie walking back and forth to refill a glass."

That's when she swings at me, an open palm coming at my face. I grab her wrist in midair. Hold it there between us. The more she tries to free herself the tighter I squeeze.

I'm much stronger than her, I realize, but this ain't about strength. I'm trying to get her to look at me. I want her to really see me for once in our lives. If she ain't gonna love me, she's gonna hate me. She's gonna feel *something*.

"Ya can't hit me, 'cause I'm grown up," I tell her. "That's how dead ya been. Ya ain't noticed."

"Let go of me."

I ain't never seen her this angry. She's getting stronger

now, twisting her forearm and pulling. She tries kicking me but I swing her away from me.

A cell phone rings, coming muffled from her room.

Calls for her are usually one-minute chats, but these last weeks they been lasting longer. And she's been talking lower than normal. Always in her room.

Suddenly I'm thinking about Brian and the call on lasagna night, when I got out of the hospital.

And what about the "No!" she screamed before I got knocked out cold? Was that panic really for me? Was she afraid I'd get hurt or afraid Brian would get in trouble?

Still clutching her wrist I ask, "You talking to him?"

"Who?" Her eyes tell me she knows who.

I let go of her hand and bolt down the hall and into her bedroom. I lock the door behind me.

"Outta my room, Marcos!"

She pounds on the door. I go through the handbag on her bed, still hoping I'm wrong. On the fourth ring I snatch up the phone.

I press answer and hold it to my ear. I wait, wrapped inside a silence so strong it might kill me.

"This call will be recorded and monitored. I have a collect call from . . ." Then I hear his voice: "Brian."

I picture his mug shot, then the mustached face I know better, seeing it close-up and twisted angry. The words come. *Dipshit. Spic. Bean nigger.* The names he called me, either shouted from the armchair or said while he hovered over me. I feel them tearing me up inside all over again.

The recording continues: ". . . an inmate at Hillsborough County Sheriff's Office."

I click off and the phone drops from my hand. The pounding on the door's fading as the room blurs. The bed, the dresser, the closet, the TV, the curtained window, everything fuzzy.

I see myself clearly though, for the first time in weeks, maybe the first time ever. The way anybody else might see me. Pathetic Marcos Rivas, needing something his mom can't give him.

After I wipe my eyes, the room snaps into focus. Again I'm hearing the door banging and rattling.

"Open up, Marcos!"

I do and shove past my mom, head straight to my own room, and lock myself in. The banging follows me, my own door rattling.

"Honey, listen! People make mistakes! Brian just made a mistake!"

Every pound on the door sucks oxygen from the room. I gotta get outta here fast, so I pop out the window screen.

I bike to the entrance of Maesta without nobody seeing me and bust a left. My direction's usually school, Brewster Park, the 7-Eleven, all the usual places, but I go left for some reason.

I see a new mural tall as me and six yards wide on the

front of a Maesta building. It's the fireball-on-a-hook guy again.

I don't want to stop but I do. The colors pull me in, and I get lost in the swirls of blue and green.

Again I feel like I know this painting, that it's for me. Focusing on it, I finally see hands in there, trying to grab at me. It's a painting of desperation. I stop being lonely for a moment, looking at it.

Then I pedal at full speed, legs pumping like rabid dogs are chasing me, the wind swirling around me. I cross at red lights when the traffic lets me, and though my thighs and calves burn I try to keep up with the cars.

After a bunch of weeks stuck inside I gotta get far from my house and can't do it fast enough.

Soon I'm on the corner of MLK, close to the hospital where I stayed and later got my stitches removed. The farthest south I've ever been. I keep riding, passing a Cuban hood where a tiny shopping center sells products in Spanish. A *mercado* advertises fruit and vegetables prices *por libra*.

How long have I been riding? Forty minutes? An hour?

I'm crazy far from home now. Stopping at red lights, I take in everything around me, the newish houses and the trees, a short pause before speeding on. I need more. Need something else.

I pass a huge park of gazebos and grills, with a playground and two basketball courts. Three kids are shooting hoops. How easy it would be to start a two-on-two, and balling would feel real good, but no. I gotta keep riding.

The sky looks bluer and brighter, the air smells salty clean, and suddenly I know where I'm going, where I been meaning to go since I left the house.

I'm heading to the water.

All I know is Clearwater Beach, which is a freeway bridge ride away. Last year I went with Ruben's family. Me and him swam and played Frisbee. Washed down sandwiches and chips with orange soda, seagulls circling overhead. But the water's what I remember the most.

The swelling waves rushed toward me. I dove through them before they crashed, or else I jumped, the cusps lifting me skyward and slowly setting me down. The water hugged me.

Worn out from swimming I floated, eyes shut, the sun warming my face, the liquid softness wrapped around me like a hug.

I wonder if the waves in Tampa are bigger than at Clearwater Beach.

With each block the yards widen and get greener. Sweat has glued my T-shirt to me.

After seven more blocks I see it, through the bloated heads of trees. The paleness of the clear blue sky blending with the grayish blue of the water.

A strong wind from the Gulf touches me. The branches of the fat trees shiver, and a palm tree reaching into the sky swoons, enormous leaves flapping.

On this side of Bayshore Boulevard stand two-story mansions behind lawns with no fences, like nobody would dare step foot on the grass, much less try to break in.

On the sidewalk, across six lanes of speedy traffic, a woman jogs, steering a three-wheeled stroller. An old man holding a leash follows a big gray dog with a fancy haircut.

When the light goes green I hurry across and let my bike drop on the sidewalk. A cement barrier made up of thousands of tiny columns runs as far left and right as you can see along the boulevard. I take a peek over it. That's a five-foot drop into the water. Under this sidewalk is a dam. I'm standing on the actual wall where the Gulf of Mexico ends.

A man with music strapped to his bicep is running this way, too focused to notice me. Water slaps against the wall and sprays up, a drop falling on my arm.

"Excuse me," I say.

The man slows until he's jogging in place. Pops out an earbud and leaves it there, bouncing with him. "Yes?"

"Where can I go swimming?"

"Well . . ." He's bobbing up and down, thinking. "There's a pool at the Y. South Himes, I think it is."

"No, in the Gulf." For some reason I point to the water. "Where can I go in?"

He stops jogging. "You can't go in there, buddy."

"I know not *here*."

I explain that I want the shore, someplace to go in the

water. Why's this taking so long? I wanna swim, dammit. He's supposed to just point.

He tells me nobody's allowed to swim in the Gulf. Besides, it's filthy. I lean over the concrete barrier for another look. Seems fine.

"The bay is for boats," he says.

He pops the dangling earbud back in and takes off down the curving sidewalk, running even faster now. Probably making up for the time he lost explaining things to dumbass me.

I ask another runner, some pretty college-looking girl who tells me the same.

I can feel a scream building up inside me but I hold it in as she runs off. Then I let it loose, a beast howl that feels like it lasts forever.

I stomp on the barrier again and again, wanting it to crumble into the bay. I scream even more, angry with it, with my mom, with Amy, with myself, still stomping and kicking. It don't even budge. It's only when I'm outta breath and when my foot is sore that I stop.

The last of the cars zip down Bayshore Boulevard, specks glinting smaller and smaller. I'm suddenly alone, all silence except for the water lapping. I can't go home 'cause I don't got one. Got nobody to talk to either. I ain't never felt more depressed in my life.

Then I remember my friend.

32

"YOU CAN'T swim naked," Zach says. "This isn't Europe."

He's holding out two swim shorts, red and blue, the same black stripe along the side.

"Bloods or Crips?" he asks.

"Crips."

Once we change and are in his backyard, it hits me I'm in a different world and it ain't just the nice pool and house. It's that I'm here as a friend, without schoolwork to do. Me and Zach are kicking it together. I'm considering this and admiring the row of bushes studded with violet flowers when he shouts "Bombs away!" and cannonballs into the pool.

I jump in after him in a crazy karate pose, a foot going for his head. He ducks under the surface to dodge it.

My sun-heated skin cools in the water. The chlorine smell tickles my nostrils.

In the deep end I slide down, become a ball, set my heels against the smooth wall and push, skimming the bottom of the ocean, a strange fish. I can hold my breath for one back and forth.

When I burst back into the world of oxygen and light, there's a whiteboy sailing through the air, feetfirst, one fist up. It's the elbow drop from wrestling. I curl my body back under the water with a splashy kick.

After messing around some more and tying twice in a swim race, we dry ourselves off. The sun's crouching behind a gray house. In the late evening light of the red sky, the tall wooden fence seems to be on fire.

In his bedroom, the freezing air makes us shiver in our goose-pimply skin.

Zach teaches me the buttons for the video game and then kicks my ass five times. With all that biking and swimming and now playing *Call of Duty*—I've forgotten Amy and my mom. Until now.

Playing our sixth game, my soldier going into some sorta warehouse, I tell Zach about the day I told Amy how I felt about her and she friend-zoned me. The words unglue inside me and I give him all the weakass details.

I'm trying something new here. I'm trying to talk to another boy about stuff that matters.

"She says we just friends," I tell him. "Which felt like she ripped my heart out, stomped on it, and then elbow-dropped it."

In the game I make a wrong turn and come face-to-face with four soldiers. Before any take aim at me I throw a grenade that blows them all to bits.

"Well done." Zack pauses the game and sets down the game controller. "But you know she didn't really rip your heart out, right?"

I almost let my head drop, but then I don't. I wanna see Zach. And I wanna be seen.

"It's still in there, man, but ya know what I mean."

"What *I* mean is that just because you love someone, it doesn't mean they'll love you back. I've been in your shoes."

Makes sense. Amy didn't do nothing to me. I did it to myself. While you expect your mom to love you, I guess it's sorta dumb to expect automatic love from anybody else.

This whole time Amy's been my friend and I been hoping for something else. She knew about Brian before anybody else. She looked out for me, brought my home-work to the hospital, and together we got our grades up. She always had my back.

Just like Obie and all my other boys.

Feels like my head might explode with that realization.

And it hits me that she never friend zoned me. *I* was the one who girlfriend zoned *her.*

I sit up as much as possible in the beanbag that looks like an orangey, half-deflated basketball. Who woulda thought I'd be kicking it here, talking about heartbreak with a whiteboy I met at a course called Future Success?

The beanbag exhales when I shift my weight. "Ya said you been in my shoes. Someone didn't love ya back? Who was it?"

A long pause and stare. He's been open about a lot of stuff but some people keep these kind of secrets all their lives. Zach gets up to close the door and sits back down on the bed.

"Yeah. Last summer at camp I liked a person who could never love me back in the same way." He ain't dying to talk about this.

Before he changes the subject I ask, "Boy or girl?"

He gets quiet for a few beats. "Are you asking me if I'm gay?"

"Yeah."

At least he's okay with me asking. Ask another kid that and you fighting.

"Yeah, I'm gay," Zach says, like he's giving up from exhaustion. "It's not something I announce though. I don't want to get tormented every day."

Poor Zach. Not for being gay but for hiding who he is. It's true he'd get tormented every day. And it don't end with the last school bell. The online bullying got so bad for eleventh-grader Eric last semester that he ended it with a whole bottle of Tylenol PM.

It hits me that even though I don't hate gay people I'm sorta part of the hate. I use "gay" like a dis. *Used* that word like a dis. I ain't doing that no more. I guess it's like people calling things "spic" or "nigger" to describe things that ain't cool.

Zach pretending to be what he ain't, hearing disses from people of all colors and ages, boys and girls. Could Zach's life suck more than mine?

"Okay, man," I say.

"*Okay?*" Zach's looking at me like my hair just turned orange. "I tell you I'm gay and that's all you can say?"

I shrug.

"Really? Some people *think* I'm gay, but you're the only person that knows."

That's really cool, him making me the first. "Thanks?"

"So . . ." Zach sits there waiting for something. "Say something, at least. What do you think?"

"That you gay?" I ask. After he nods I say, "I don't care. Like who you want. I don't get why anybody cares."

"Me neither."

I down the rest of my lemonade and set the glass aside. "If anything, all guys should be gay," I say. "That'd be a perfect world. I'd have a girlfriend for sure, a new one every day."

When he cracks up, I realize it's sorta funny and start laughing too.

"Yes!" Zach says, trying to regain his breath. "And it would mean more guys for me!"

I laugh harder and harder, my first laugh in weeks.

Laughing with my whole body so that even my arms and legs are trembling.

Riding home through the dark streets I feel a strange peace come over me. I cut across the lit-up field of Hanna High, wondering why the lights come on at night when school is out and if the bugs in the grass can sleep anyway. That's when I remember the fish. I panic.

Since my idea's too scary for second thoughts I hurry up and do it. I get to the fence behind the cafeteria and start climbing. This is crazy. Have I lost my mind?

There ain't no barbed wire up here but a loose wire on the pole snags the back of my jeans. I nearly bust my ass.

I hop down and walk onto the strip of grass. Here, between two rows of classrooms, nobody can spot me checking for an unlocked window.

From inside the rooms you push the window open, but out here there's nothing to grab on to and pull. I stick the back of my fingers hard against the panes, my nails gripping underneath the metal. I pull hard, ignoring the pain. It takes five classrooms before a window wiggles. With both hands, using all my strength, I get it to budge and then it flies open, almost hits me in the face.

Moonlight comes through the windows, brightening the speckled floor. I can just barely make out the whiteboard and the map of the world. This is Ms. J's classroom.

I look at my desk. My *old* desk. That's where I stood

and applauded Ms. J that day she cried. I ain't so good about that now.

I head to the principal's office, the weak glow of my cell lighting the way. Though I know I'm doing the right thing, my heart's beating fast.

As usual, the office blinds are down. Why have a see-through wall if you ain't never gonna see through it? I press my phone against the glass to light up the office some. I see a corner of Principal Perry's desk and where the tank . . .

It's gone. Someone must be taking care of the fish at home for the summer. I look at the emptiness on top of the two-drawer file cabinet.

How stupid to come here and check on them. What was I gonna do? Take them home? Break in every night to feed them? Like they'd still be alive with school shut down for weeks already.

I go back to Ms. J's classroom. Standing in the front I picture these desks full. I see what the teacher used to see. Students staring back. All the pranks come back to me, especially the last one, Ms. J walking out, her face streaked with tears.

In my own life, dealing with hurt, I sometimes wonder, *Why me?* But I've hurt people. I shoved Zach on the cafeteria floor before I knew how awesome he was. I made Amy cry after the school play 'cause she had a boyfriend. And that's just the stuff I can remember. And that's just in the last school year.

When I spot the red whiteboard marker I get an idea. I uncap the marker and start writing.

You're the nicest teacher in the world and if I could take your class again I'd sit in the front row with my ears wide open and never prank you or make you sad in any other way. Thanks for everything.

A short message but to the point. I set the marker down. Reading it again, I realize something's missing. Not my name—that's proof I broke into the school. I pick up the marker again and sign: *A Future Success kid.*

When I reach the top of the fence on my way out I hear a loud bark. My heart damn near leaps outta my chest and I hang on tighter to the bar between my legs. Down there is the homeless dog. It wasn't a mean bark. Come to think of it, barks from him ain't ever been mean, and again I wonder why I'm so scared of dogs.

I ain't never really met one before him. Maybe that's why. Nobody has a dog in Maesta and strays don't ever pass through, as if they know better.

From up here he looks small.

"Be cool," I tell him, and slowly climb down so I don't scare him away. That's right, *I* don't wanna scare *him.*

I hop down and he backs off. When I crouch and snap my fingers he hurries over all amped like a little kid dismissed for recess. He sniffs my hands and circles around me, nose ruffling the longer blades of grass.

I'm petting him and he lets me. His fur's mostly soft but you can feel dirt in there too. I scratch behind his ears and rub his head. But what shoots his tail into the air is my hand running over his short fur. It's wagging so much it might fall off. I pet him like that for a while, his eyes blinking slower with each stroke.

I don't got food but I got love. Got enough love for a zillion dogs.

Wondering where I can find some grub I remember the Burger King nearby, all those trash bins.

The sound of whistling cuts through my thoughts.

The dog barks and takes off. I follow, rounding the gym. I slow down when my eyes meet hers.

Right there, in the middle of the lit field, is Amy. I take my time walking toward her. What should I say? Will she even talk to me?

"Hi," I say, a little nervous.

"Hey," she says, in a sorta nice way. "What're you doing here?"

"Cool. You're talking to me." I try not to act like the happiest person alive.

She shrugs. She pulls out a plastic bag from the side pocket of her cargo shorts, opens it wide, and sets it on the grass. The dog attacks the food right away, gobbling up the pasta and bits of chicken, crunching on the bones.

"You been feeding him?"

"Just since school's been out. The janitor usually feeds him."

I smile at that. I used to see him feed the dog too.

She plops down on the field, knees pointing to the sky, hands clasped over her shins. I sit down too, the grass moist beneath me. The sprinklers musta been on earlier.

"I get where ya coming from now," I say. "About us not being together like that, and it's cool with me."

She nods.

"Well, it ain't *totally* cool yet, but I get it. I really do."

"So we're still friends?"

"Of course."

I tell her I never had a friend who's a girl before, and that I shoulda appreciated what I had. "I like the idea of a girl who's a friend. Friends last. Girlfriends, from what I've seen, don't."

"That's right."

"Plus you can help with the new freshman girls in September," I say. "They gonna try to use me for my hot bod and I'm gonna need advice, from the female point of view."

She laughs. "I got you."

Hidden in the grass, something tiny that either flies, jumps, or crawls gets to buzzing at a high pitch.

For now, I skip over my weeks of depression and the shouting at my mom and tell her only about the crazy afternoon, my idea to swim in the bay.

She makes fun of me for that and we laugh. Just what we need, more laughter to push our fight away.

Amy tells me about her *soul-searching*. No kidding. She actually uses that word. She's had some sorta boyfriend since sixth grade, says she only felt good about herself when a guy was with her. She's talking in her super grown-up way.

"Now I gotta do *me*," she says. "Isn't that how you guys say it?"

"Been listening to hip-hop?"

She smiles. "I gotta figure myself out. I'm not totally ready for this stuff."

"What stuff?"

"The crying over a broken heart, the worrying about the future, and all the grown-up stuff."

I laugh. I can't help it.

"What's so funny?"

"Not ready for grown-up stuff? You, Amy, are the most mature fifteen-year-old in the world."

"Not by choice. You know, I've thought the same about you."

Crappy lives have matured us, I guess, but I remember being a little kid and loving it. This is something me and Amy got in common, even more important than the Future Success program and our worthless moms and the assholes they love. It's something I got in common with every teenager and grown-up on the planet. We was all tiny once.

I notice a new mark on Amy's sneakers. She's added an *E*. It now reads *I ♥ ME*.

"I miss being little," I tell Amy. "Though we didn't have nothing figured out back then either, nobody expected us to."

She does something really dope, the kind of amazingness I never thought possible. She puts her hand on my shoulder and says, "I feel you."

Them three words, I decide, are my favorite of all time. They should be everybody else's too. They strong enough to kill loneliness.

I tell her about home, the fakeness of the last two months, and how the truth came out this afternoon with a phone call. "I don't trust her no more. But I'm over caring about it."

Tough guy words, but they true for once, even if it hurts me to say them. I got no family. Not that I ever had much, just two ladies, my mom and her mom, who mostly ignored me.

I'm so beat that I lie down, the moist grass cooling my back. Amy also stretches out. We lie here, silent.

The world feels perfectly beautiful, and not only the grass down here or the stars in the black sky, them tiny specks of light, and the half-moon burning whitely, low and watching, but even the school buildings and fluorescent lights and all the power and phone lines stretched down the street, connecting houses and people, making electricity and communication possible.

Sure, ugliness prowls the world, always finds me somehow, but I don't feel none of it now. And when I do, 'cause I will at some point, I'll know I don't deserve it. That it ain't got nothing to do with me.

"What you got going on for tomorrow?" Amy asks.

I guess she wants to hang out. I'd like to but don't know if that's a good idea right away.

"Listen, I think I need some time to deal with other stuff. I need a month. Maybe more? Sometime this summer, I hope."

Confusion on her face.

"I just wanna make sure I don't think of ya in that other way. It's dope kicking it with ya but it's also a little weird right now and I don't want it to be."

A sudden wind knocks a rope of hair over her eye. When she tucks it behind an ear, and I think the beauty of her fingers doing that might kill me, I know I'm making the right choice to not see her for a while.

"I feel you," she says.

33

I WAKE up sore as hell. Last night I collapsed on my bed, unable to move, but didn't realize it'd be permanent or nothing. After wiggling my legs, sore from yesterday's Tour de Tampa, I slide them over and get up all slow. That's when I notice a type of package on my dresser. Also a slip of paper on top. At first I think it's a shopping list, 'cause my mom sends me to the store to fetch groceries. But no. It's a note, written in her loopy cursive.

Marcos,

I'm sorry you dont got the mom you deserv. I never had a good mom and dont no how to be one. It takes all I got to just deal with being me, and I dont like being me very much. Your old enogh to understand you wernt planned, and while your grandma said I might feel different when you was born, that hasent happened yet. Your also smart enogh to no is not your fault. So I wont try to tell you that I change or that I'll start making good desishuns or anything like that. You just need to see me as a bad mom and forget it and I'll keep making sure your taken care of in other ways. And I hope to have the money for your sneakers by the end of july. Also, this package came for you.

So there it is. All I been thinking about my mom on a piece of paper. I flip it over. There's nothing else. What was I expecting? *Love, Mom?*

My whole life hoping and waiting. What a waste!

Enough, I tell myself. I crumple the note up and toss it into the trash. Enough.

The package is just a big white envelope, magazine thick. The top left corner reads *Mr. Henry Breckner,* with the school's address. Could it be about what I missed at the Future Success ceremony? I rip into it to find a picture frame. Inside it there's a certificate. It says *Certificate of Awesomeness* in big fancy letters and there's my name, Marcos Rivas.

In smaller words it says, *For completing the Future Success program and proving himself worthy of the nomination. For proving that he always had the fire in him. For being unstoppable.*

That's pretty cool. Dorky, yes, but cool. I can't wait to hang it up.

There's also a sheet of paper in the envelope. A handwritten note.

DEAR MARCOS,

    I'M SORRY THAT YOU DIDN'T COME TO THE CEREMONY SO I COULD GIVE THIS TO YOU IN PERSON. THE SURPRISE WAS THAT A FEW TEACHERS AND MYSELF RAISED ENOUGH FOR PIZZA AND VIDEO GAMES AT MCALLY'S FAMILY FUN. IT WAS NICE FOR ALL OF US TO BE THERE TOGETHER. I FINALLY GOT TO KNOW MY STUDENTS A LITTLE, WHICH I ENJOYED, AND I HOPE THEY ENJOYED IT TOO.

    ANYWAY, NEXT YEAR I'LL HAVE A NEW GROUP OF FS STUDENTS AND YOU'RE WELCOME TO COME AND VISIT ME ANY TIME YOU'D LIKE.

                    SINCERELY,
                 HENRY BRECKNER

Water's spraying down on my head when I hear some sorta tapping. I tighten the shower knob off and listen. Today I ain't ignoring nobody.

Tut-tut-tut, tat-tat. I know that knock and the voice that says, "Open up, bitch!"

I throw open the shower curtain and wrap the towel

around my waist, don't bother rinsing out my shampooed hair. Skin all slick and dripping, I rush to open the front door.

"Obie!"

I hug him. It ain't no half-hug shoulder bump with a quick back slap back but the real deal, both arms around him.

Obie laughs. "You got me wet."

I go rinse out my hair in the bathroom sink, dry off, and put on some shorts. Then hurry back to the living room.

He tells me he came by yesterday afternoon. At Art's they kinda had a party, put money together to buy hot dogs, buns, and chips. Sucks I missed that.

I ask him about juvie.

"Mostly it was Ping-Pong and basketball."

He tells me the cell was a room with a door and window he could open. He tells me that for the first weeks he didn't have internet access.

"I finally wrote ya though," he says. "A buncha times."

"Sorry." What else do I say? How can I explain I ain't left the house in weeks?

I'll just explain it. If I could talk about my heartbreak with Zach I can tell Obie, my best boy.

"I haven't been . . . "

Just then the door opens and in come Art and Jason. Art turns the armchair around and drops into it. Jason's on the floor, forever his favorite seat. Though a little more than a year has gone by since Brian moved in, since my boys could kick it here, you'd think no time has passed at all.

Art turns to me. "Where ya been?"

An obvious first question. I ain't come up with good excuses and now, on the spot, everybody eyeing me. I can't even think up a bad excuse.

"Crazy, man," I say. "I ain't even trying to get into it right now. Wassup with you two?"

"We thinking about balling."

"Kinda early," I say, "but I'm in."

Obie nods all hard. "My game's tighter than ever. Get ready for the pain."

Though I gotta put on a shirt, socks, and kicks, I don't move just yet. I wanna hear about what I missed last night.

They tell me they balled as usual. Then, when Art's mom went to work the late shift, they got together on his back porch, so many people hanging and listening to music they had to make two trips to the store for more soda and chips.

"Still can't believe Tonya's sister is pregnant," Obie says.

Getting the news just now, I can't believe it neither. The girl's thirteen. Jason and Art nod, already cozy with the information.

They tell me about Joe. On Tuesday night, cops rolled up while he was with his boys, drinking Schlitz around the bumping Mazda, too drunk to cut out. Nobody knows what he got charged with.

Art gives me a wide-eyed look. "And Whiteboy ain't told you."

"That's right," Jason says. "Last week I'm at the corner, you know, by the lot where we used to bat rotten oranges? I'm about to cross when two *chicos* run up on me. The one that looked familiar busts me in the kidney and jacks my bike."

"They took your new Mongoose?"

"No, bitch, my Harley. What you think? It was ya boy from Asha's party."

Hardstare. I remember. I tell Jason I'm sorry.

He shrugs. "Ain't your fault."

My boys have been trying to track Hardstare down. When I mention that Asha's cousin might know where to find him, Art gives it straight, like a TV news guy. Days after school ended, Asha ghosted him.

"What?"

"Yeah. Then yesterday I find out she's with someone else."

"Who?"

He shrugs. "Not a broke-ass nigga. Believe that."

Sucks for Art. Asha was great, and I ain't just talking the obvious reasons like how hot she is. We'd all been jealous of our boy.

I spent so much time hermitted in this house I might as well have been in juvie too.

Art's really relaxed on that armchair, one of my favorite people right where an asshole used to sit. Jason, quiet as ever, is stretched out on the carpet, propped on his elbows. They came to drag me and Obie to the court and look at us here, still chilling, in no rush. Or maybe basketball was just a reason to stop by and talk without having to say *Hi, I wanna talk.*

Ruben comes through the door all happy like we called him over for breakfast. "I got big news, bitches."

"Ya finally discovered your penis?" Art says. "That it ain't just a pimple on your nutsack?"

"Ha ha. Check this out."

"Hold it right there." Jason puts his hand out like a traffic cop.

Ruben's energy drops. "For what?"

"Just hold it right there."

We laugh at that.

Since there's always a reason Ruben gets amped, we wanna catch his excitement, but we also like to keep on edge like this, about to burst.

"Just listen." He's grinning from his own good news.

I fake confusion. "Ya mean *right now?*"

"Is that what ya want, Ruben?" Obie says all slow. "Ya want us to listen right now?"

"Fuck off." Ruben gets quiet. After putting up with a few more jokes he begins. "So me and my cousins are swimming in their subdivision's pool and this hot girl goes to chat up my cousin Elisa. I catch her checking me out and later ask Elisa to hook me up. Anyway, she just called to give me the number. Cuban girl, Sara's her name."

Obie turns to us. "Let's think about this . . . Why would a girl give Ruben the Sex-God Cuban her number?"

"Probably a fake number," Art points out.

And the joking shoves Ruben outta his storytelling again. Obie mentions a recent published study, that 97 percent of girls named Sara are lesbians.

"Ruben," I say. "I don't consider it big news that a Cuban lesbian gave you a fake number."

He's fed up now, turning red with rage. "Here I am trying to hook my boys up, but each one of ya can kiss my ass."

He heads to the door mumbling, "*Qué clase de come-mierdas.* This is the last time I—"

When we shout apologies he turns around smiling, unfazed. "So we texting and vibing with each other and she mentions she's hitting the mall later with some friends, and I text back that me and my boys should meet up with them." He's beaming like someone just handed him a trophy.

"And?" Obie's getting impatient.

"And she said yeah! We meeting some hotties today!"

We flip the hell out, game-show style, jumping and shouting our fool heads off. I rush Ruben and put him in a headlock. With them weights he lifts, he's got no problem pushing me off, but here comes everybody to tackle him.

It feels like summer's really started now.

34

IT'S STEAMY-BATHROOM hot, the high sun hating on us, not caring we got miles to go and shouldn't get sweaty. We coasting over our own shadows, five guys on three bikes, taking turns pedaling each other.

Jason's standing on my rear pegs, hands on my shoulders, his eyes all over the street. In these miles we covering he's trying to spot one of the thieves or his bike.

We switch after another block and it's me back here with the nice view. You notice the city more this way, when you ain't gotta focus on not getting killed, on the cars zipping past, damn near grazing you.

At the mall entrance, after we chain our bikes, Obie breaks into his celebratory dance, the one you see on the basketball court. I get amped too. Amy and I are friends now, that's cool. So now I can maybe meet a new girl who could like-like me, for real.

Ruben hits up Sara to check if they already waiting at the fountain.

Up ahead! Is that? Of course it fucking is. Art's ex-girl sitting with some guy on a bench. A kid with crazy bank. The parents with bank, I mean. Even if that earring's cubic zirconia, not diamond, and that chain gold plated, not solid, them red and white kicks tell you everything—an edition of Jordans so limited I ain't ever seen them before.

Any second now Art will notice Asha and the new guy, there they are, closer all the time, the sweet couple too sophisticated for ice cream cones. They eating outta cups with miniature pink spoons. Asha sees us and lowers her head. I can *feel* Art noticing her. Something in the air changes.

"Keep walking," I tell him, and make sure he does.

Picture that—us about to meet girls and we get arrested for stomping on a kid.

"Ain't sweating it," Art mutters as we move on.

Ruben pockets his cell. "Sara's here with five friends," he says, looking more at Art. "They waiting."

We joke about Obie needing a girl badly after months without even looking at one.

But when we peep them up ahead, the two girls sitting on the fountain's edge, the other four standing, I know it ain't gonna happen.

The girls are pretty, two of them banging hot, but check out their clothes, the proud way they sit, the way they stand, the way one girl twirls her hair and the other holds her handbag, dangling from a forearm. They don't carry themselves like Desiree and them. I can tell we ain't got nothing real in common with these girls. Sara and her one friend clutching an iPhone are both Latinas, but the wrong kind.

The blonde with her legs crossed, the first to notice us, flinches like we jumped out from behind a bush. All of us understand, boys and girls, that this is a huge fuckup, that not a damn thing's gonna happen. Except for Ruben who's still smiling.

"Hey, Sara," he says, leaning in for a traditional cheek kiss.

She takes a step back. Art turns away. It really is hard to watch.

They been texting so this is the first time she's heard his ghetto voice. At the pool where she saw him he was just another boy in swim shorts. Now she understands who he really is.

"Hi there." Her singy voice matches her summer dress and sparkly flip-flops but not her skin.

The seated girl looks at my shoe. Fuck! The tape's poking out! I almost bend down to fix it but that'll get more attention. She turns to her friend who also looks down at my shoes. They barely crack a smile. They saving this story for later, when they'll wear themselves out from laughing.

Sara glances at her friends before speaking. "We're

going to some stores right now, okay?"

"Yeah!" the nearest friend says, coming alive. "We have to check out some sales!"

Sara turns away from Ruben. "See you around."

"Hang on," Ruben says.

But they take off, all six of them, designer flip-flops slapping the hard floor.

We in Foot Locker checking out the new kicks, the fitted caps, stuff we can't buy.

Good thing we hanging around the mall for a while. Leaving right away woulda bummed me out even more.

Ruben's scoping out the jerseys in the back. Art's asking a worker if they got any free stuff, making Jason and Obie laugh.

Even after we visit a clothes store where the jeans cost three hundred dollars, and then head into the weird tech shop, I keep thinking back to them hot girls, the way they looked at us, at Art and Obie especially. Like we was dog shit they stepped in.

A man with a name tag necklace hurries over like we called him. Obie sets down the wireless headphones he was trying out.

"Where to now?" he asks.

Ruben shrugs. "Let's go."

So we heading out. I'm more than ready. Let's delete this mall visit from our brains, the sooner the better. You can't let that shit break you. It's something I've learned. You gotta forget the mean laughs and stares, the heads turning away, all the hurt that comes your way, but there's a problem: I suck at forgetting.

Hell, I'll remember them girls in ten years, in fifty years. I'll remember them when I'm laid up in my death-bed with tubes in me.

Walking through the mostly empty mall, past the fountain again, my boys still got the tall stride, but I know they won't forget this neither.

I see through their faking.

We step into the bright afternoon, the humidity on us like we uncovered a pot of rice.

Ruben's slump is worse than when we found out Le-Bron was leaving Miami. Something's nudging me to talk. I did it yesterday with Zach and Amy, so why not here?

I watch Ruben unlock his bike and ask him, "Ya feeling okay, man?"

My other boys are watching too.

He turns to us, straightens, and when it seems he's gonna say something, he don't. Then, a second later, he does: "They walked away 'cause I'm short."

None of us laugh. None of us call him gay or a pussy. Ruben just gave a confession and I respect him, the guts it took to say that.

I look Ruben straight in the eye. "It ain't you, man. Girls like that don't want guys like us."

My boys nod right away.

Jason says, "We poor."

"Whiteboy's right," Art says. "Imagine one of they dads opening the front door and finding a Maesta kid."

Obie sets a hand on Ruben's shoulder. "We can't even afford to take them to the movies."

Ruben nods.

Ain't no secret that being Maesta poor makes us different from them girls and everybody else, but saying it out loud changes them as much as it changes me. We been hanging out for years, talking about everything except what's going on deep down with us, so now it's like we just became friends for real.

That openness I had yesterday with Zach and Amy I could have with my own boys, so something else gets knocked loose inside me. Right here, outside the Florida Palms Mall, while the sun's baking our heads, I decide to go for it.

"You know these last weeks I ain't hung out? I was bummed about Amy."

I fill them in on Amy since the beginning, how I was thinking love when it was just friends. I tell them everything straight through to the end.

"If I ever get sad like that again, I ain't staying in my house. Fuck that. One of you is gonna get a visit from me."

"Sure," my boys tell me. "Anytime."

This letting go of what's inside is totally unlike me, and

you know what? I'm totally into it. I think they might be too.

I turn to Obie. "That's why I didn't write these last weeks."

"Don't sweat it."

Art lets out a big sigh. "Seeing Asha with Rich Boy didn't surprise me none."

"At least you've had a girlfriend," Obie says.

"Yeah," Ruben says.

"There's always next year," Art says.

Although it's hard to tell if this cheers anybody up, he's right to be thinking of the future.

"That's the good thing about being totally screwed," I tell them, and can't help but smile. "Things can only get better for us."

Everyone laughs except Art.

"As long as we don't go to jail," he says.

"We ain't going to jail," Obie says. "That's over with."

"Or as long as we don't get shot," Art says.

Cedric on the sidewalk, blood oozing outta a hole in his stomach.

"We ain't getting shot and we ain't going to jail," I say. "We getting outta Maesta."

"How's that?" Jason asks.

Only Obie knows where I'm going with this.

"You got a rich daddy?" Obie asks. "Can you rap? You good enough to play for the NBA? How you gonna get out?"

"School," Ruben says.

"High school ain't got shit on me," I say. "I'm crushing it the next two years and then I'm making college my bitch."

Which gets them all laughing again, even Art.

A security guard comes outta the mall to stand in the thin strip of shade in front. I'm so not in the mood for this today. I'll ignore him. I turn to Jason who's silent as always, a faraway look on his face.

"You okay, man?" I ask him.

"Yeah, Whiteboy," Art says. "Why don't ya ever say shit?"

Jason shrugs. Without a bike, he don't make much sense. Even when he's balling with us it seems like he should be off on his own, wheeling around and doing tricks. It's his thing.

Ruben says, "What ya think about all this?"

Jason takes a deep breath. He looks down like he dropped something, then raises his eyes to us. "I want ya guys to stop calling me Whiteboy."

The rest of us look at each other. I wonder who started the nickname years back. Maybe that's who better apologize. I guess it don't matter though. We all do it.

"I won't say it again," I say.

Obie pats him on the back. "That Whiteboy stuff was just messing around."

Could it be that Jason has something else in common with me and don't like being alone? Maybe feeling different's the reason he spends so much time by himself.

I ask, "Ya know we down for ya, right?"

"Uh-huh, sure."

Jason don't say nothing for a while and then pulls from his back pocket a rectangle of paper and holds it out. "Since we talking about stuff . . ."

I unfold the paper and find a drawing done in colored pencils. Graffiti on paper. I recognize the style from the buildings in Maesta. In my hands is a future mural! Right there, at the bottom corner, is the hook and fireball tag.

While the rest of us go stiff from shock, Art's freaking out. "You? No fucking way! That really you?"

Jason tries to fight off a smile but cracks a small one.

Ruben does his lunatic laugh and Obie snatches the paper from my hands to admire it up close. The eyes in the middle of the splotches of color are gray, like Jason's, and shaped the same way. Then I figure something else out.

"The tag," I say. "It ain't a fireball. It's the sun! The hook's a J, right?"

Jason nods, but my boys ain't getting it.

"J," I tell them, and point to the bluish hook at the bottom right corner. "Sun." I point to the ball of fire burning around it, orangey red. "Jason."

"My boy's an artist!" Ruben shouts.

"Keep it on the down low," Jason says, unable to hold back the smile. "I ain't trying to go to juvie for this."

"Your secret's safe," Ruben says. "Don't worry."

Jason folds the paper and pockets it. "I ain't worried."

That's right, no need to worry.

Know why? 'Cause other people will let you down, will rat you out, will make promises they don't keep or turn away when you need them most. But me and my boys? That ain't how we roll.

How lucky that I been tight with these guys all my life. With friends like these, who needs family?

Suddenly I'm thinking about the courts in Chapa Park. Ain't played there for months. Ain't balled in weeks.

"Chapa Park, bitches," Ruben says, like our brains are attached.

"Crazy," Obie says. "I was thinking the same thing."

I laugh. "Me too."

Jason and Art are nodding.

"It's time to go," the security guard says. "No loitering."

He's walking over to us, wide shouldered, his uniform almost looking like a real cop's, except there's a walkie-talkie where the gun's supposed to be.

The sun's burning us up and we got our bikes pulled from the rack so we obviously leaving.

"We going," Obie says. "You see we going."

"Alright, then." He stops halfway between the doors and us. "I'm waiting."

I point over to the entrance outside Macy's, where three white kids are still hanging out, one of them leaping off a bench. "Tell *them* to hurry up and go. They been there forever."

"I'm telling *you* to hurry up and go."

Art gives us the look. Though his fuse is crazy short, he won't do nothing unless we do. And we ain't in the mood for that. But we can mess with this guy.

Obie starts it off by nodding to Art. I scan the parking lot, then turn to the security guard again. Ruben undoes his watch and puts it in his pocket. Jason creeps one step forward.

The man uncrosses his arms, dropping the badass cop act.

We stand here staring him down. But we ain't gonna do anything.

"Not as tough as ya think," I say, and we all laugh as we hop on our bikes and ride off.

35

SMOOTH, UNCRACKED courts, gleaming white back-boards, and orange hoops with nets. At Chapa Park, when you hit a swish, you ain't gotta imagine the sound. Four courts are separated by two wide strips of grass shaped like a plus sign. There we let our bikes fall and face the superstar court. College boys today, some in the green and yellow gear of the University of South Florida.

When Ruben calls downs the shooter laughs. You'd think he was right outta boot camp with that haircut, but the green tee with the yellow USF initials tells you he belongs with the others. The only black person on the court, a guy with tiny dreads, points to the court behind us, where the players are around our age.

We all shake our heads. We got downs right here.

The other player with the headband, the tannest one, might got some Latino in him. There's also an Asian guy and the rest are white. They look like a Gatorade commercial.

The players keep on with the game.

They balling damn good, but see how they don't feel each other right? The new-sneakers guy keeps falling for pick-and-rolls, and Tiny Dreads throws passes that hesitate. Individual skill they damn sure got but ain't playing like a true team.

When Soldierboy takes another jump shot the game's over.

"Let's do this," Art says.

We hop up right away. Before the winners are done high-fiving, we standing on the court, looking wrong in baggy jeans.

Tiny Dreads gestures to the older guys who just showed up.

"Fuck that," I say. "We had downs first."

"Seriously? This is ridiculous," Tiny Dreads says. "You can play over there."

I get all up in his face. Actually, all up in his neck. He's really tall. "Ya scared of getting stomped?"

Obie snatches the ball from Soldierboy and sits on it. He and the rock ain't going nowhere.

The college guys look at each other.

"Whatever," Tiny Dreads says, shaking his head. "Throw it in."

We take off our sweat-soaked shirts and toss them on

the grass. Except for buff Ruben, we look smaller, super skinny next to the Gatorade guys. Don't give a fuck though. I'm feeling strong.

"I'm covering the Rastafari princess," Art says, his game face on.

"Okay," I say. "I got G.I. Joke."

On the sidelines, Obie grips the ball over his head. "Try to score at least one shot, college bitches. Make this less embarrassing for yourselves."

The moment the ball's thrown in, we bringing it hard. We in synch with each other, perfect gears in a shiny new machine.

Whether it's offense or defense, me and my boys know how our teammates will react. Sometimes what's gonna happen I can see in my brain for half a second before it actually happens, like déjà vu.

I got the same fire on the court as always, and how dope that I brought that same fire to my last weeks of school. Gonna bring that same fire everywhere I go.

I sink a perfect jump shot over Soldierboy.

After ten minutes into this the Gatorade guys have gone from annoyed to pissed. They trailing, 6–2. Even joggers have stopped to watch us, the wrongly dressed ghetto kids dazzling on the court.

Every score, stolen ball, or blocked shot's followed by talk like *How did that one feel?* and *Why ain't nobody filming this?*

Now Art swipes the ball from Tiny Dreads, all of us changing direction, and no-look passes to Obie who spins around Headband Boy before tossing it to Ruben who sinks an easy one off the board.

These college chumps got nothing on us. Before they know what came at them we one point from winning.

"10–5, bitches," Ruben says. "Game point!"

We take our spots on the other side of the court.

Soldierboy dribbles toward me, us head-to-head. I ain't letting him pass. When he goes up for a jump shot, I'm there too, going even higher, and slap that ball right outta his hands.

The spectators *oooo* as the ball bounces off the asphalt and rolls onto the grass.

"Go home and practice," I tell him.

"Hey, watch it." His freckled face is inches from mine.

Tiny Dreads comes through to put an arm between us. "Take it easy," he tells me. "It's just a game, bro."

But we one point from victory and it feels like much more than a game. Winning's everything.

So when Soldierboy throws the ball back in, me and my boys keep playing like our lives depend on it, 'cause they sorta do.

You see, the girls we like are into other guys, and we so poor we got no seat for our bikes or enough shirts for all the days of the week, or we so jinxed we get two bikes ganked in eight months, or we got moms who don't care or who call the cops on us, and we forever dealing with bullshit 'cause we from a place where good things rarely happen.

But here, on the basketball court, winning's possible.

Here you can take to the air like some heavenly being and snatch a rebound off the rim, like Obie just did, and bullet-pass it to Jason who dribbles twice before side-arming it to me.

And you can hustle, like I'm hustling now, cutting past one guy, spinning around another, nothing before me but hoop, moving full speed toward it, all eyes on me, the baddest Maesta kid you've ever seen, and you can leap into the sunlight, release a layup so amazingly perfect that I know, that everybody knows, even before the ball leaves my fingertips, that it will be the winning point.

ACKNOWLEDGMENTS

THIS BOOK would be nothing more than a file in my laptop's memory if not for my wonderful agent, Louise Fury.

It would be less readable if not for the insight of my editor, Jessica MacLeish.

I am honored to be working with Rosemary Brosnan and the entire team at HarperTeen. Thanks for loving this book, for working with me to keep it authentic, and for always having my back.

Thank you, Annie Berger. You read this quickly, loved Marcos, and it changed my life in the best way.

Marko Fong, Chaz Josephs, John Knight, Lorena Cassady, Sydney Oliver, and Anne Louise Pepper were my first readers, and gave me helpful notes on the manuscript. Thank you.

The kindnesses of two friends when I needed it the most helped me focus on my first draft. Thank you, José Pareja and Paul Jove.

I am especially grateful to my sisters, my mother, and Tío Pedro for their love and encouragement since the beginning. You believed in me and it meant more than you will ever realize.